TRUE TALES *of* Kentucky POLITICS

TRUE TALES *of* Kentucky POLITICS

Bombast, Bourbon & Burgoo

Berry Craig

The History Press

Published by The History Press
Charleston, SC 29403
www.historypress.net

Images are courtesy of the author unless otherwise noted.

First published 2009
Second printing 2011
Third printing 2012
Fourth printing 2012

Manufactured in the United States

ISBN 978.1.59629.636.7

Library of Congress Cataloging-in-Publication Data

Craig, Berry.
True tales of old-time Kentucky politics : bombast, bourbon, and burgoo / by Berry Craig.
p. cm.
ISBN 978-1-59629-636-7
1. Kentucky--Politics and government--1792-1865--Anecdotes. 2. Kentucky--Politics and government--1865-1950--Anecdotes. 3. Political culture--Kentucky--History--Anecdotes. 4. Politicians--Kentucky--Biography--Anecdotes. 5. Kentucky--Biography--Anecdotes. I. Title.
F455.C73 2009
976.9--dc22
2009004390

Notice: The information in this book is true and complete to the best of our knowledge. It is offered without guarantee on the part of the author or The History Press. The author and The History Press disclaim all liability in connection with the use of this book.

To my parents, Sue and Berry Craig Jr., and my wife,
Melinda Hocker Craig, who all said I should write a book.

Contents

Introduction

Television tamed Kentucky politics, which was famously fired by the "Three *B*s"—bombast, bourbon and burgoo. Today, most Bluegrass State politicians are fine-tuned to the sound bite. It takes too long to spin a political yarn on TV. Few pols probably know how anyway.

For most of its history, Kentucky was celebrated for leather-lunged, silver-tongued orators such as Henry Clay, John C. Breckinridge, William O. Bradley, A.O. Stanley, Ed P. Morrow, Alben Barkley and John Sherman Cooper. When Senator Wendell Ford retired in 1999, that noble line ended.

Before TV, Kentuckians swore by, swore at and sometimes punched their politicians. Ante-TV, Kentucky politics was the best free show in the state. From Paducah to Pikeville, politicians battled with bombast, bourbon and burgoo.

Bombast

Bombast might be defined as the political art of employing many words to say little or nothing. Bombast gives special meaning to the last lines of "In Kentucky," Judge James H. Mulligan's immortal 1902 poem:

Mountains tower proudest,
Thunder peals the loudest,
The landscape is the grandest—
And Politics—the damnednest
In Kentucky.

So is bombast. Examples are plentiful, and none is better than a supposed oration by a legendary legislator named Mullins.

Mullins's yarn was a favorite of William O. Bradley, who in 1895 was elected Kentucky's first Republican governor. Dubbed "Billy O'B," the Garrard County native had few peers at stump oratory.

M.H. Thatcher included "Mullins' Famous Speech" in his book *Stories and Speeches of William O. Bradley*, which was published in 1916. Mullins, according to Thatcher, lived "years ago in a certain county bordering on the Kentucky River." Mullins was a "unique character" who was "not as eloquent as [Henry] Clay, nor yet as erudite as [Daniel] Webster." Even so, Mullins "possessed a sonorous voice, accompanied with great oratory, which made him famous for miles around."

Mullins delivered his "famous speech" after he returned home from Frankfort, where he had gone by steamboat. "Feller citizens," he began,

> *When you elected me to the Legislature, I wished that I mout have the tallest pine tree that growed in the mountings, so that I might strip the limbs from same and make it into an enormous pen, and dip it in the waters of the Kaintuck River and write acrost the clouds, "God bless the people of ——— County."*
>
> *Arter you elected me I went down to Frankfort on the Blue Wing, and as we wended our winding sinuosities amidst its labyrinthian meanderings, the birdlets, the batlets, and the owlets flew outen their secret hidin' places and cried out to me in loud voices: "Sail on, Mullins, thou proud defender of thy country's liberties."*
>
> *When I reached Frankfort, I went up into the Legislatur hall and thar spied many purty perlicues a-hangin' on the ceiling to pay for which you had been shamefully robbed of by unjest taxation. When matters of small importance were before the body I lay like a bull pup a-baskin in the sunshine, with a blue-bottled fly a-ticklin' of his nose; but when matters of great importance come up I riz from my seat, like the Numidian lion of the desert, shuck the dew drops from my mane, and gave three shrill shrieks for liberty.*

BOURBON

In early Kentucky, many a vote was swayed, outright bought or rewarded with whiskey. Campaign expenses included barrels of booze, "the spirit of democracy," when the Bluegrass State was young.

A local officeholder defined a successful politician as a man who "could drink Grog all day without getting drunk," according to Bernard Mayo's book *Henry Clay: Spokesman of the New West*. Victory at the polls awaited almost any office seeker who could "drink whiskey and talk loud with the fullest confidence," said Mayo, quoting Bluegrass State newspaper editor Amos Kendall's famous observation. (Kendall was later an important member of President Andrew Jackson's Kitchen Cabinet.)

Yet today, most Kentucky counties are "dry," meaning that it is illegal to sell or drink alcohol in their confines. Politicians generally avoid imbibing in public, fearing that they might offend members of some conservative Protestant congregations, Baptists among them, which declaim the demon rum.

But a metal marker near the Royal Spring in Georgetown, the Scott County seat, says that the Reverend Elijah Craig, Baptist, "first distilled bourbon whiskey on this site in 1789." The tablet, placed by the Bourbon Institute, explains that the Virginia native siphoned the spring's "fine limestone water…to develop the first sour mash process in the production of bourbon." Craig also founded Georgetown, according to the plaque.

The parson was dubbed "the Father of Bourbon." However, Craig "or any of a number of other distillers may have produced the first bourbon," the *Kentucky Encyclopedia* cautions. "It is doubtful that the name of the first distiller of bourbon whiskey will ever be known."

Craig was a controversial man of the cloth, but not just because he squeezed corn, according to Ann Bevins, a Georgetown historian. "Elijah Craig had an acrimonious personality that got him into a lot of trouble for making 'hasty remarks' about his fellow Baptist clergy," she said. "Baptist sources also insist that Craig was overly inclined to serve 'mammon' in deference to his higher calling."

Born in the Old Dominion about 1743, Craig became a Baptist minister before he migrated to Kentucky in the 1780s. He became a pioneer distiller, though he possibly discovered the technique for making bourbon by accident, according to the encyclopedia.

Many, if not most, Kentucky Baptists foreswear bourbon as the devil's brew. Hence "the distilling industry has taken delight in pointing to a Baptist preacher as the inventor of its prime product," the encyclopedia notes.

Old Baptist isn't a bourbon brand, but Elijah Craig is. Baptists regularly tippled in Craig's day, Bevins said. "There was no conflict at that time regarding the distilling and drink of spirituous liquors unless the drinking was in excess," she explained.

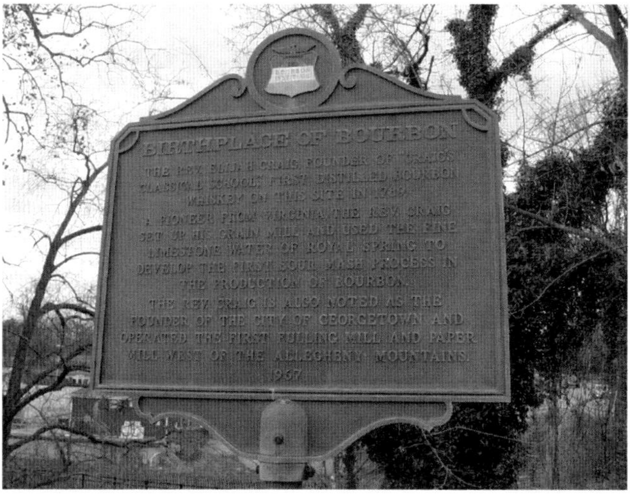

Baptist minister Elijah Craig is credited with distilling the first batch of bourbon on this site in Scott County in 1789.

According to Bevins, Craig's newfangled whiskey was said to be so smooth that the Kentucky legislature supposedly considered outlawing it. "Allegedly, one lawmaker worried that the mellowing process would cause 'even women to drink it.'"

The whiskey Craig was credited with creating stayed legal and ultimately became known as bourbon, apparently named for Bourbon County, where early distillers were plentiful. The "Birthplace of Bourbon" sign also says that the Father of Bourbon, who died in 1808, started Craig's Classical School "and operated the first fulling [wool processing] mill and paper mill west of the Allegheny Mountains," also in Georgetown.

Twenty-two years after Craig went to his reward, George D. Prentice, a sober-minded New England native, crossed the mountains and settled in Louisville. He was appalled at politicians who bought votes with booze. Prentice, who became editor of the conservative and Whig *Louisville Daily Journal*, lamented that on election days in Kentucky "whiskey and apple toddy flow through our cities and towns like the Euphrates through ancient Babylon," according to *The Rampaging Frontier: Manners and Humors of Pioneer Days in the South and the Middle West* by Thomas D. Clark.

Politicians could tell whether they got what they paid for. In the old days, elections in Kentucky lasted three days and were decided by voice voting. There were many liquor-fired fights around the polls, even in Frankfort, the state capital. Prentice witnessed such a brawl between one of the Salt River Roarers, a gang of toughs, and another drunken roughneck he nicknamed "Bullet Head." After the long, bloody fight, Prentice said that he walked away "a confirmed believer in the doctrine of total depravity," Clark wrote.

Sometimes conscience attacks panged Kentuckians who sold their votes for booze or money, or both. That's understandable. A special morality was at stake. When you sold your vote, were you conscience-bound to stay bought?

A Graves County voter wrestled with that conundrum. He was bought, fair and square. But he still wanted to vote for the other candidate.

He could probably have gotten away with it. This was in secret ballot times.

What was he to do? He asked a trusted relative for advice.

The relative suggested, "Go ahead, take his money. Drink his whiskey. Then vote for whoever you damn well please. But pray the SOB gets at least one vote in your precinct."

Over in eastern Kentucky, a father lit into his thick-skulled son for selling his precious vote for four dollars, according to *A New History of Kentucky* by Lowell H. Harrison and James C. Klotter. The going rate, Pap yelled, was seven dollars and a half pint of Heaven Hill bourbon.

BURGOO

Generations of Kentucky politicians knew that the true path to voters' hearts ran through their stomachs. Servants of the people plied the citizenry with burgoo.

"A 'burgoo' is a cross between a soup and a stew, and into the big iron cooking kettles go, as we sometimes say in Kentucky, a 'numerosity' of things—meat, chicken, vegetables, and lots of seasonings," recalled Vice President Alben Barkley of Paducah in *That Reminds Me*, his memoirs. The concoction became so synonymous with politics in Kentucky that a political rally that featured the stew was called a "burgoo." Barkley described himself as a frequent partaker when he "toured the political hustings in certain parts of the Blue Grass State."

There were big burgoos everywhere. One of the biggest was at Mayfield, the Graves County seat, on October 17, 1931. The occasion was a visit by Judge Ruby Laffoon of Madisonville, the Democratic gubernatorial hopeful in that grim Depression year.

More than eight hundred gallons of burgoo were brewed in fifty-two iron kettles over smoky blazes that made the *Mayfield Messenger* mindful of "Chicago after a certain historic cow had kicked over a lantern and set fire to two thousand acres of property."

Dr. Bow Reynolds was the "master of affairs and chief cook," according to the paper. Twenty volunteers helped, tending kettle fires and preparing the ingredients for the burgoo blowout: 1½ tons of beef, ½ ton of pork, 40 bushels of potatoes, 40 bushels of onions, 480 cans of tomatoes, 40 bushels of carrots, 1,200 roasting ears (of corn), 40 gallons of peas, a bushel of red peppers and a gallon of garlic.

Approximately seven thousand people showed up to hear Laffoon and Albert B. "Happy" Chandler, the Democrat running for lieutenant governor, give speeches and sample the free burgoo at the old Mayfield High School football field.

Reynolds and his aides began brewing the burgoo the Thursday night before the Saturday rally. Burgoo central was the Jackson Purchase stockyards west of town. "Down through the middle of a large covered stock pen is a long alley extending from one end to the other," a *Messenger* writer described the scene.

> *On either side are stalls, formerly occupied by livestock but now inhabited by peelers of potatoes, carrots, onions and various other vegetables. In the alley is a row of forty old-fashioned iron kettles. Some are as large as a barrel in circumference, and others are larger.*

The paper's scribe found the "pots boiling…and they had just sent for a dozen more." The *Messenger* suggested that "no one person probably will ever know how many different things are in a batch of burgoo." But the paper assured its readers that the burgoo contained nothing metallic because "all cans have been removed from around the tomatoes before they were dunked." The *Messenger* described the stew as "a six-course dinner all boiled in one…With proper seasoning burgoo can't be anything but good and nutritious."

The burgoo was served in pasteboard cartons with slaw and bread for sides. It took three hours to feed the multitude, the *Messenger* reported.

"There was plenty to eat," the paper also said. "Scores of gallons" went unconsumed because Reynolds and his helpers made enough burgoo for ten thousand. Reportedly, the leftover burgoo was given to a local charity for feeding the hungry.

While Reynolds's recipe called for beef and pork, frontier burgooists used wild game. It has been suggested that the varmint version of burgoo was palatable only with a bourbon chaser.

CHAPTER ONE

"Ed Morrow Plain Makes Me Sick to My Stomach"

Bombast, bourbon and burgoo blend into one of the most famous Bluegrass State political stories. Evidently, the tale is true.

It dates to the 1915 governor's race between Democrat Augustus Owsley Stanley of Henderson and Republican Edwin Porch Morrow of Somerset. Both were masters at bombast and were fond of bourbon and burgoo.

Stanley might have had the oratorical edge. "Sufficiently fired with Old Crow, he could make himself heard across the narrow waist of Kentucky," Thomas D. Clark wrote in *Kentucky: Land of Contrast.* He liked to introduce himself as "A.O. Stanley of Henderson, Kentucky, where the cypress trees grow so tall that the topmost branches tickle the feet of Democratic angels in Heaven and the roots go so deep that they scratch the bald heads of Republican sinners in Hell."

Author and humorist Irvin S. Cobb, born in then devoutly Democratic Paducah, defined Heaven as "a place which went unanimously Democratic every fall, because all the Republicans had gone elsewhere."

The 1915 campaign's high point—or low point—came on a day as hot as blue blazes. Where is evidently forgotten, or the location is simply not included in the story. Anyway, Stanley and Morrow were to take the stump together. Both stalwarts supposedly fortified themselves with ample burgoo and bourbon.

Morrow went first. By all accounts, his speech was reasonably coherent. When Stanley's turn came, the spirit was willing but the body balked.

He stood up, aiming for the rostrum. His knees buckled. His head swam. His stomach revolted. He threw up.

Stanley was sunk, Morrow was sure. The Democrat might as well quit the campaign. But "surrender" wasn't part of A.O. Stanley's vocabulary.

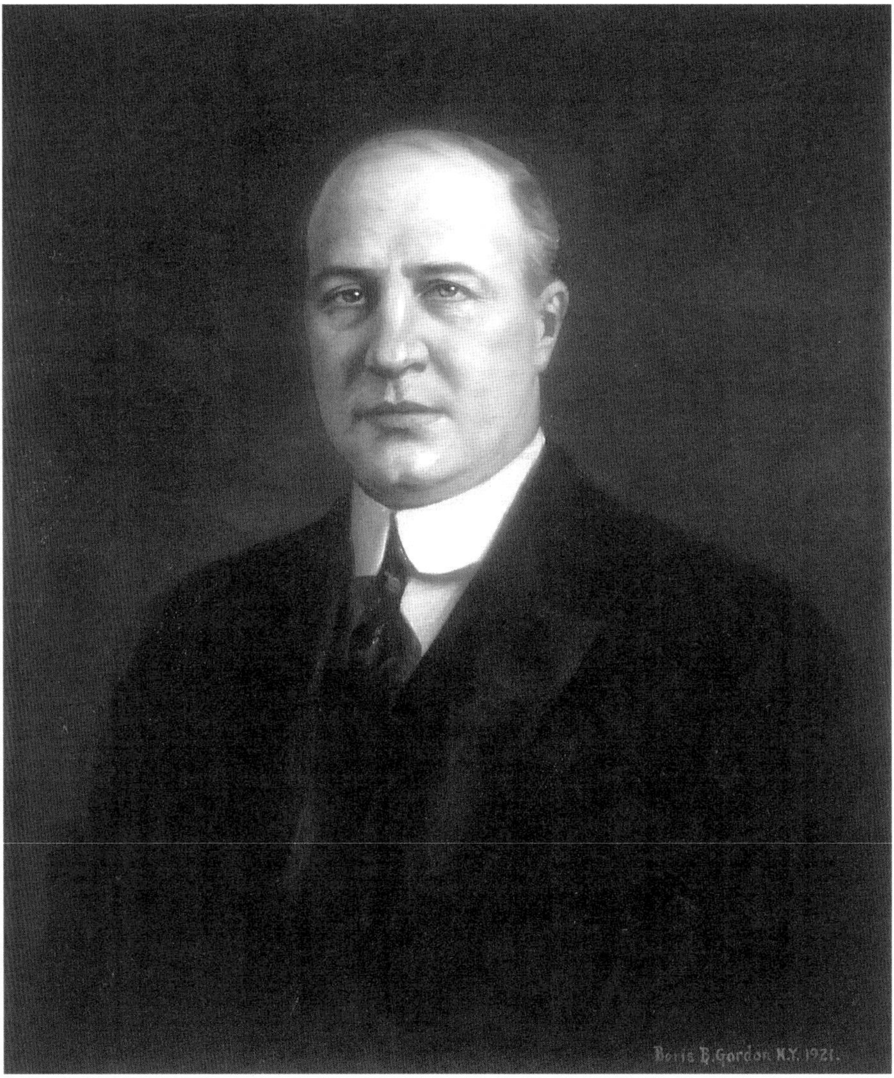

Edwin P. Morrow (1877–1935). *Courtesy of the Kentucky Historical Society.*

He wiped himself clean. Though still in an alcohol fog, he staggered to the podium. "That just goes to show you what I have been saying all over Kentucky," Stanley declared, according to *A New History of Kentucky*. "Ed Morrow plain makes me sick to my stomach." (There are slight variations on Stanley's comeback in other sources.)

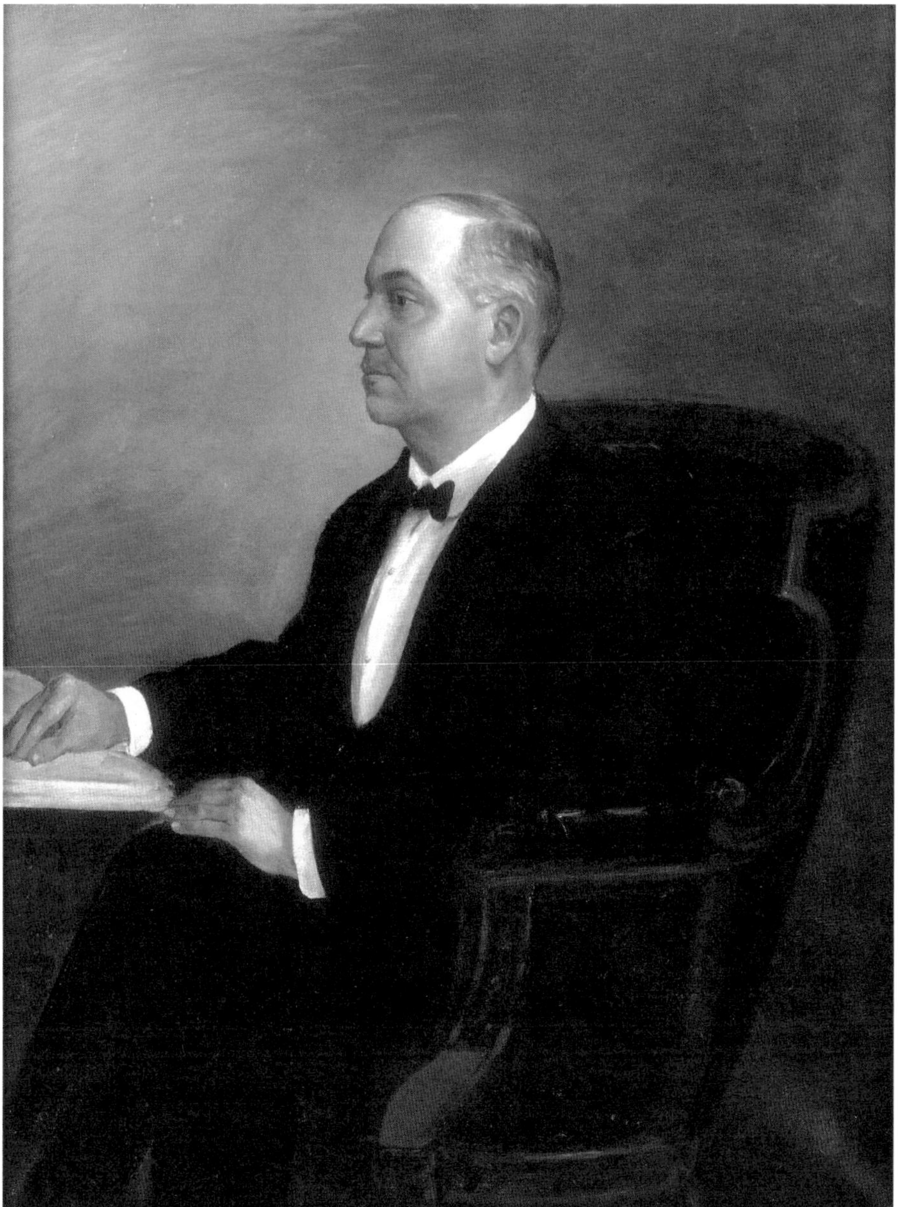

Augustus O. Stanley (1867–1958). *Courtesy of the Kentucky Historical Society.*

Stanley got elected. Once out of office, he reputedly told a gathering of other ex-governors that there were two things he'd had in life and never wanted again: "Gonorrhea and the governorship of Kentucky."

"Poetry Is Loved and Lives Forever"

James H. Mulligan of Lexington was a lawyer, legislator, journalist, judge, orator and diplomat. But he is best known for penning "In Kentucky," the poem that proclaimed politics "the damnednest in Kentucky."

"Judge Mulligan was famous for poetry and prose that was pedantic and purple," said Ron Bryant, a historian and writer who is manager at Waveland Historic Site in Lexington.

A Literary History of Kentucky by William S. Ward claims that "In Kentucky"

> *has no doubt been more widely circulated than any other poem written in Kentucky. It was set to music and chanted, it was widely reproduced in newspapers and journals, it was quoted in the halls of Congress and read into the Congressional Record, additional verses were composed and publicized, at least fifty parodies in most states of the United States have been traced, and withal, it is estimated, well over a million souvenir postal cards have been sold with the verses printed on them.*

Ward also cited Mulligan's poem in *The Kentucky Anthology: Two Hundred Years of Writing in the Bluegrass State.* "Seldom has hyperbole reached such dizzying depths of bathos," he wrote.

Judge Charles Kerr's *History of Kentucky* says that "In Kentucky" "has girdled the globe. At least one Kentuckian has heard it chanted in the shadow of the Egyptian pyramids by a nomad of the desert and a thousand poets have parodied it."

Born in Lexington in 1844, Mulligan "often stumped the 'deestrick' for the democratic tickets of his day and generation," the history book explains. "He became widely known as a stump speaker, and lucky was the political aspirant who had Mulligan for his champion."

All along, Mulligan wrote poetry. He introduced "In Kentucky" at a 1902 dinner for state legislators hosted by the Lexington Chamber of Commerce.

Mulligan was one of several speakers. According to *A Literary History of Kentucky*, local newspapers reported that he "spoke wittily for about fifteen minutes on his earlier membership in the Kentucky General Assembly; then he 'drew from his pocket, as if drawing a deadly weapon, a dangerous looking manuscript' and read the poem":

"In Kentucky"

The moonlight falls the softest
In Kentucky;
The summer days come oft'est
In Kentucky;
Friendship is the strongest,
Love's fires glow the longest;
Yet, wrong is always wrongest
In Kentucky.

The sunshine's ever brightest
In Kentucky;
The breezes whisper lightest
In Kentucky;
Plain girls are the fewest,
Their little hearts the truest,
Maidens' eyes the bluest,
Their little hearts are truest
In Kentucky.

Life's burdens bear the lightest
In Kentucky;
The home fires burn the brightest
In Kentucky;
While players are the keenest,
Cards come out the meanest,
The pocket empties cleanest
In Kentucky.

Orators are the grandest
In Kentucky;
Officials are the blandest
In Kentucky;
Boys are all the fliest,
Danger ever nighest

Taxes are the highest
In Kentucky.

The bluegrass waves the bluest
In Kentucky;
Yet bluebloods are the fewest (?)
In Kentucky;
Moonshine is the clearest,
By no means the dearest,
And yet, it acts the queerest,
In Kentucky.

The dove's notes are the saddest
In Kentucky;
The streams dance on the gladdest
In Kentucky;
Hip pockets are the thickest,
Pistol hands the slickest,
The cylinder turns quickest
In Kentucky.

Song birds are the sweetest
In Kentucky;
The thoroughbreds are fleetest
In Kentucky;
Mountains tower proudest,
Thunder peals the loudest,
The landscape is the grandest—
And politics—the damnedest
In Kentucky.

Kerr's *History of Kentucky* concluded that

> *it is as the author of the "new" Kentucky home "In Kentucky" that Mulligan's most lasting fame is founded. The law is musty; politics is a bore; diplomacy is another form of deception; but perfect poetry is loved and lives forever.*

CHAPTER TWO

Governors and Their Kith and Kin

"The Militia Pig"

Apparently nobody knows where Governor Isaac Shelby might have buried the Militia Pig, a War of 1812 veteran like Kentucky's first chief executive, who adopted her. "I don't think the pig is in the Shelby family cemetery," said Brenda Willoughby, retired manager of Constitution Square State Historic Site in Danville. "But I would assume if it was a pet, it would have been buried somewhere."

Willoughby also oversaw the Isaac Shelby Cemetery State Historic Site. That property is in Lincoln County, five miles south of Danville, seat of Boyle County. The plot contains the graves of Shelby, his wife and others.

A sign at the site is silent about the sow. The porker purportedly retired "in ease and indolence" on Shelby's farm, according to Lewis Collins's 1847 *Historical Sketches of Kentucky*.

In 1813, the Militia Pig joined Harrodsburg-area recruits heading to Canada to battle the British. The men hadn't gone far when they spied "two pigs fighting, and delayed their march to see it out," Collins wrote. The winner fell in with the troops, waddling all the way to the Ohio River, opposite Cincinnati, where the soldiers crossed on a ferryboat. The sow swam the river and waited "on the other side until the whole *cortege* crossed over."

The volunteers eventually rendezvoused with Shelby, a Revolutionary War hero who was elected governor in 1792, when Kentucky became a state, and won another term in 1812. He got special permission from the General Assembly to lead Bluegrass State soldiers in the War of 1812.

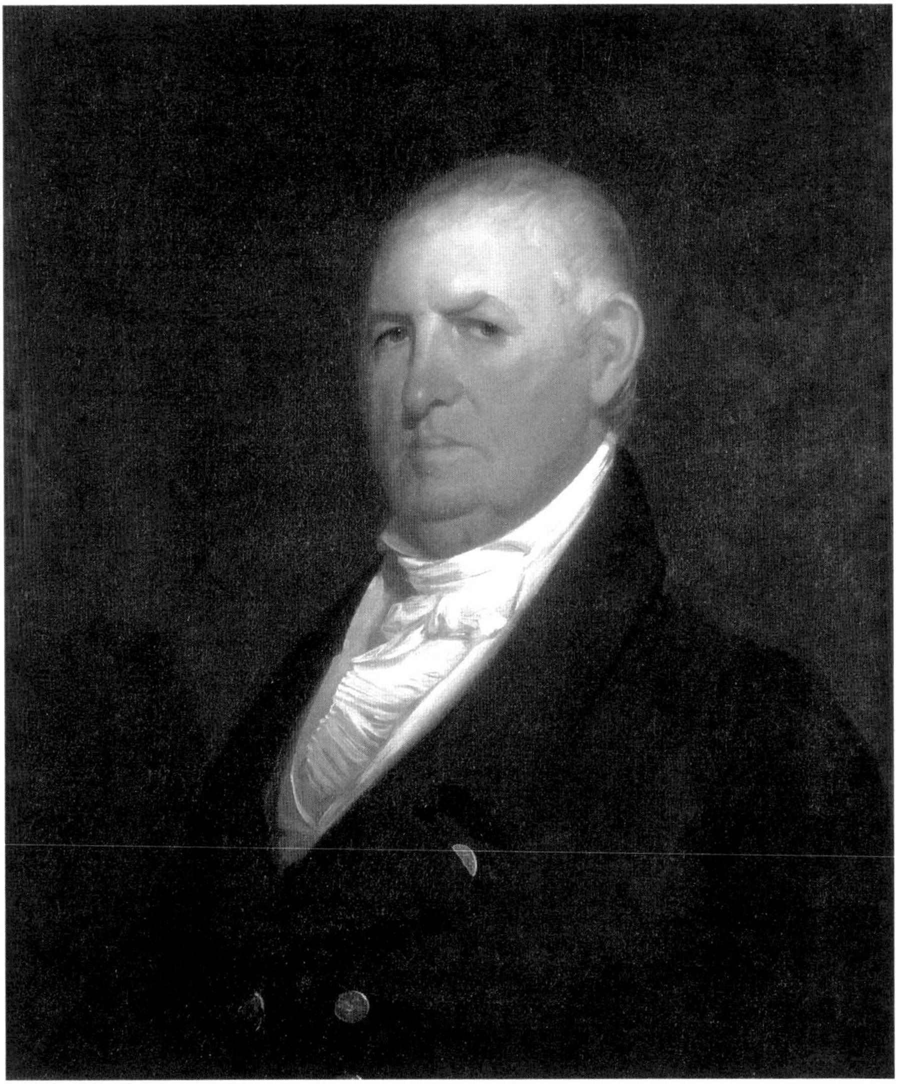

Isaac Shelby (1750–1826). *Courtesy of the Kentucky Historical Society.*

"On the whole journey, as the men grew more familiar with their comrade, it became a pet, receiving a full share of the rations issued to the soldiers, and destitute as the troops found themselves at times of sustenance, no one thought of putting the knife to the throat of their fellow soldier," Collins wrote.

When the troops reached Lake Erie, the ham on the lam refused to go to Canada. Some of the Kentuckians attributed her behavior not to cowardice but to "*constitutional scruples*," the historian explained. Collins claimed that the hog knew no "*militia pig*" could be forced to fight on foreign soil against his—or her—will.

The American army won some battles in Canada, but it lost the campaign and retreated stateside. When the Kentucky troops recrossed Lake Erie, they found the pig "ready to resume her march with the rest," Collins wrote.

It was winter, which made the trek to Kentucky doubly difficult for the dispirited soldiers. They were cold, tired and hungry. Even so, nobody turned the sow into pork chops.

The Militia Pig "suffered greatly on its homeward march" and finally collapsed at Maysville, Collins wrote. Shelby left the pig "in trusty hands" to recuperate. He later summoned the swine, which apparently spent the rest of her days in an earthly hog heaven.

A Governor's Son Cheats the Hangman

Most Kentucky history books barely mention the 1825 trial of Francis Baker's killer. But few other trials have created a greater sensation in the Bluegrass State. Few Kentucky courtrooms have ever had a higher-profile defendant. In the dock facing capital murder and robbery charges was Isaac Desha, son of Governor Joseph Desha.

"It was certainly one of the most interesting, most intriguing and most political trials in Kentucky history," Ron Bryant said. "It also helped give Kentucky justice a really bad name."

The trial, held in Cynthiana, the Harrison County seat, was marred by charges of gross judicial misconduct. A second trial, an attempted suicide, a deathbed pardon and a political scandal followed.

In 1824, the year his father was elected governor, Desha, who lived in Fleming County, was accused of slaying the unsuspecting Baker, a visitor from Natchez, Mississippi. Desha purportedly stole his victim's money, too. "It was a particularly gruesome murder," Bryant said. Baker's body—bloody, beaten, stabbed and stripped—was found in a gully six days after Desha allegedly killed him with a leaded horsewhip and a knife.

Isaac's attorney was a headliner himself, the famous duelist and soon to be U.S. Senator John Rowan of Bardstown. Rowan got the trial moved to what he hoped would be friendlier territory—Cynthiana. The governor lived on a farm outside of town.

Joseph Desha and John Rowan were friends. So were the governor and the presiding judge, George "Peg Leg" Shannon.

In 1825, a Harrison County jury found Desha guilty of robbery and murder and fixed his punishment as death. Shannon ruled that the evidence was tainted, set aside the verdict and ordered a new trial.

Shannon was accused of thwarting justice to save the criminal son of his political crony. Some angry citizens burned the judge in effigy. Desha was retried in Cynthiana in 1826. The judge and jury were different; the verdict and sentence were the same.

Desha tried to cheat the hangman by cutting his own throat with a straight razor. Doctors were sure that Isaac would not survive the self-inflicted wound. Believing his son was near death, Desha pardoned him. Miraculously, Isaac lived.

"The pardon was quite a bombshell," Bryant said. "Based on all the evidence, Isaac was guilty as sin. After the trial, a lot of people got the idea that in Kentucky if you were well-connected, you could get away with murder, literally."

Governor Desha survived the stormy scandal that the pardon brewed, finished his four-year term and retired to his Harrison County farm. Shannon moved to Missouri. Isaac purportedly disappeared. "It was claimed that he changed his name and left Kentucky," Bryant said.

"Supposedly, he was seen in New York City, Honduras and California," he added. "Then, after a while, the whole episode was all but forgotten. It was relegated to the dustbin of Kentucky history."

"I Feel as David of Old Did When He Was Told of the Death of Absalom"

The slaying of General Ben Hardin Helm moved President Abraham Lincoln to tears. "I feel as David of old did when he was told of the death of Absalom," Lincoln lamented, according to *Chickamauga: Bloody Battle in the West* by Glenn Tucker.

Helm, who is buried in Elizabethtown, where he lived most of his life, was the Kentucky-born president's brother-in-law and the son of Governor John Larue Helm.

Ben Hardin Helm died fighting Lincoln's soldiers in the Civil War. "Lincoln showed a kindness and patience toward the Helms that went beyond magnanimous," Bryant said.

After Helm's death, Emilie Todd Helm, the general's twenty-six-year-old widow, spent about a week at the White House. Her visit raised some capital city eyebrows and hackles.

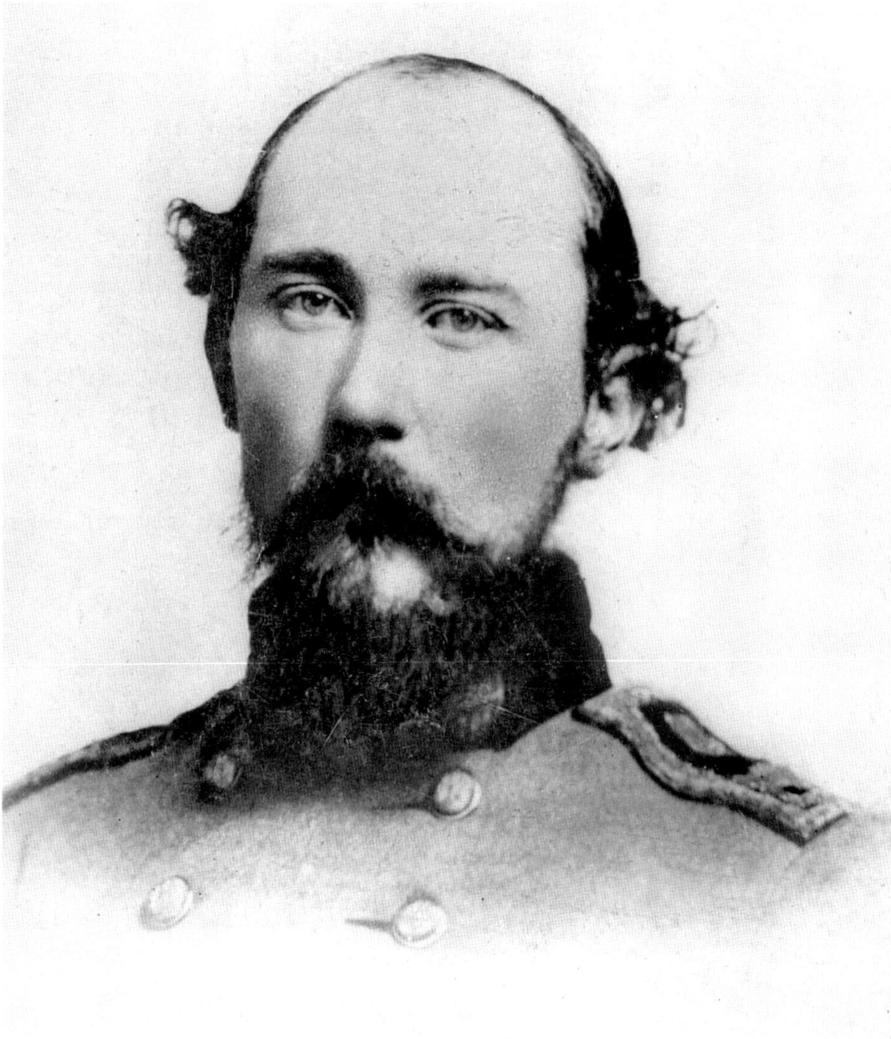

Benjamin Hardin Helm (1831–1863). *Courtesy of the Kentucky Historical Society.*

Emilie Todd Helm was Mary Todd Lincoln's half sister. Lincoln was so fond of Ben Hardin Helm that he tried to make him a Union army major.

A Southern sympathizer, Helm declined Lincoln's offer. "He raised the First Kentucky Cavalry for the Confederate army," said James Ramage, a Northern Kentucky University historian and author.

Helm, thirty-two when he died, was a West Point graduate whose father was Whig governor of Kentucky from 1850 to 1851. Reelected as a Democrat in 1867, he died soon after taking office.

Ben Hardin Helm was mortally wounded while commanding the storied Kentucky Orphan Brigade, an infantry outfit, at the battle of Chickamauga, Georgia, on September 20, 1863. What happened next "is the stuff romantic legends are made from," Bryant said.

Emilie had followed her husband south with their two daughters, according to R. Gerald McMurtry's book *Ben Hardin Helm: "Rebel" Brother-in-Law of Abraham Lincoln*. She and the children were in Alabama when she took them to Atlanta to oversee the general's burial.

Elizabeth Todd of Lexington, Emilie's stepmother, secured a pass from Lincoln to go to Atlanta to fetch her grandchildren and the widow Helm. On the way back, Yankee troops detained Emilie when she refused to swear an oath of allegiance to the Union, McMurtry wrote.

Knowing that he had the president's sister-in-law in custody, the officer in charge telegraphed Lincoln. "Send her to me," the commander in chief responded.

THE TRAITOR GOVERNOR

He was scorned as the traitor governor who helped "blacken the history of Kentucky." Even so, his death was widely mourned in Georgetown, his home. "Few in the community did not share in the grief over the loss of a friend and neighbor," Lowell H. Harrison wrote of George W. Johnson in the *Register of the Kentucky Historical Society*.

Johnson was Kentucky's first Confederate governor, but not for long. He fell in the Civil War battle at Shiloh, Tennessee. "Johnson's arm was so crippled that he couldn't even load a musket," said John Robertson, an author and historian from Paducah.

Johnson was born near Georgetown in 1811. He helped organize a rump Rebel state government behind Confederate lines at Russellville in 1861. Rebel-held Bowling Green was the Confederate "capital" of Kentucky.

"This government had no legal standing," said Robertson, who taught history for many years at Paducah Community College, now West Kentucky Community and Technical College. "It did not represent the true feelings of most Kentuckians."

The Johnson government, denounced as treasonous by the Union-majority legislature in Frankfort, retreated from Kentucky with the Confederate army in early 1862. Despite his age and disability, Johnson fought as a volunteer at Shiloh.

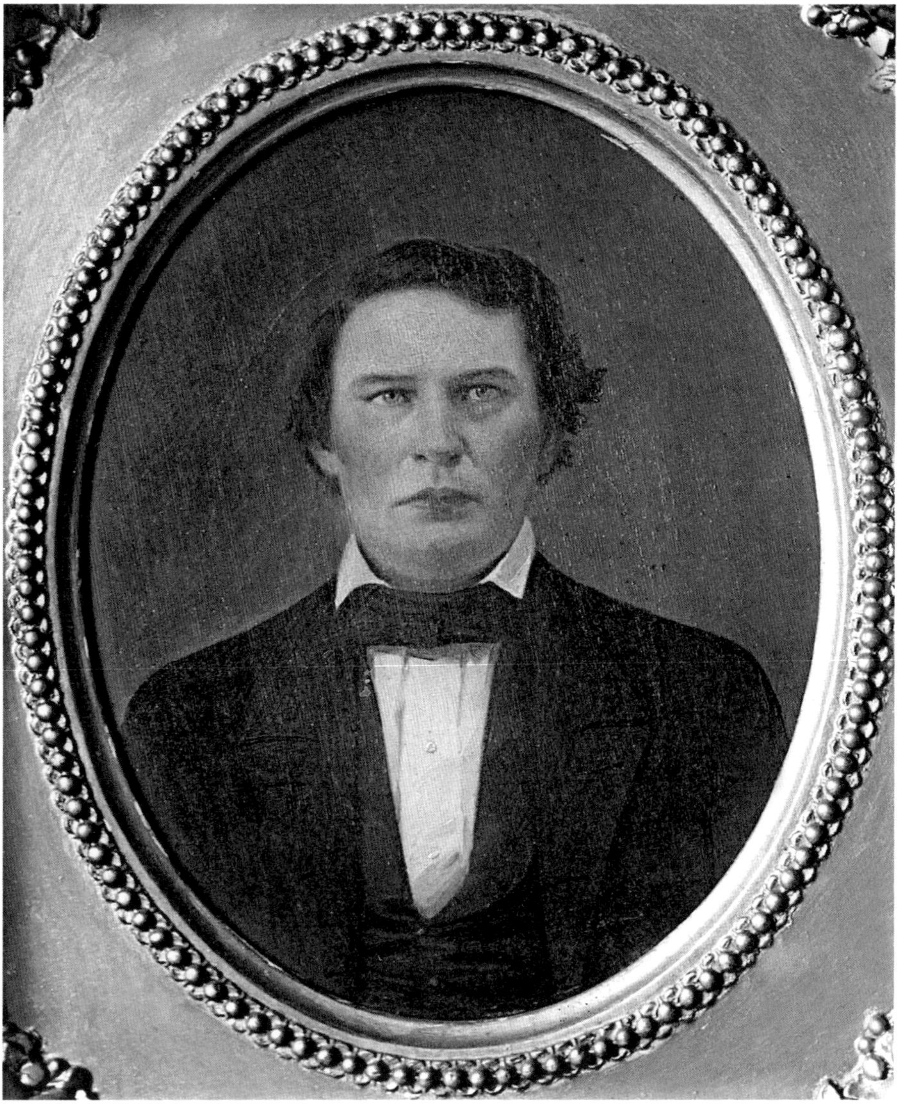

George W. Johnson (1811–1862). *Courtesy of the Kentucky Historical Society.*

When the Yankees shot Johnson's horse out from under him, he joined the Fourth Kentucky Confederate Infantry as a private. "I am determined to share the dangers of the battle with these boys," Harrison quoted Johnson. "They are my friends and relatives, and I feel better with them."

His comfort was fleeting. On April 7, 1862, when the Union army won the two-day battle, Johnson "was struck by two bullets, one in the right thigh, the other in the abdomen," wrote Harrison, a retired Western Kentucky University history professor. "He lay unattended on the littered battlefield until the following day."

Union General Alexander McDowell McCook of Ohio recognized Johnson. He rushed the wounded governor to a hospital boat on the nearby Tennessee River and ordered doctors and a chaplain to attend him, Harrison wrote.

Johnson died on April 8. Two Kentucky friends in Union blue—Colonels John Marshall Harlan of Frankfort and James S. Jackson of Hopkinsville—helped speed Johnson's remains, which were packed in salt, to Georgetown for interment in the city cemetery, Harrison wrote. "Buried here are Kentucky governors Joseph Desha and James F. Robinson, Confederate Gov. George W. Johnson..." reads a state historical society marker at the old graveyard. Confederate sources predictably praised Johnson, Harrison wrote. "More impressive were the tributes from his political enemies," the historian added. Harrison cited George D. Prentice, the fiercely pro-Union editor of the *Louisville Daily Journal*. Johnson "was a rebel in arms, and he deserved his fate," Prentice penned. "But we have a kind regard for him. We knew him well...Terribly was he deluded, but we have a heart-tear for him."

"One of the Greatest Outrages on a Free Election Ever Perpetrated on Any State"

A state historical marker at Wickland, Charles A. Wickliffe's mansion in Bardstown, is silent about "the teeth of bayonets and the threat of arrest" that purportedly prevented him from serving another term as governor.

The 1863 Kentucky governor's race, held in the middle of the Civil War, "was one of the greatest outrages on a free election ever perpetrated on any State," the *Vincennes Sun* editorialized from neighboring Indiana, according to *The Civil War and Readjustment in Kentucky* by E. Merton Coulter.

To help ensure Wickliffe's defeat, a Yankee general resorted to martial law. A Union colonel stopped Wickliffe from voting. He warned the candidate that "no poll should be open for him," according to Lewis and Richard Collins's 1873 *History of Kentucky*.

Before the Civil War, Wickliffe was a Whig state legislator, member of Congress, lieutenant governor, governor and postmaster general. He sought the governorship in 1863 as a Peace Democrat.

Kentucky was a Union state. But by 1863, many citizens had soured on the Civil War, America's bloodiest conflict. Hence, the Union army brass in the Bluegrass State was worried that the antiwar Wickliffe might be elected.

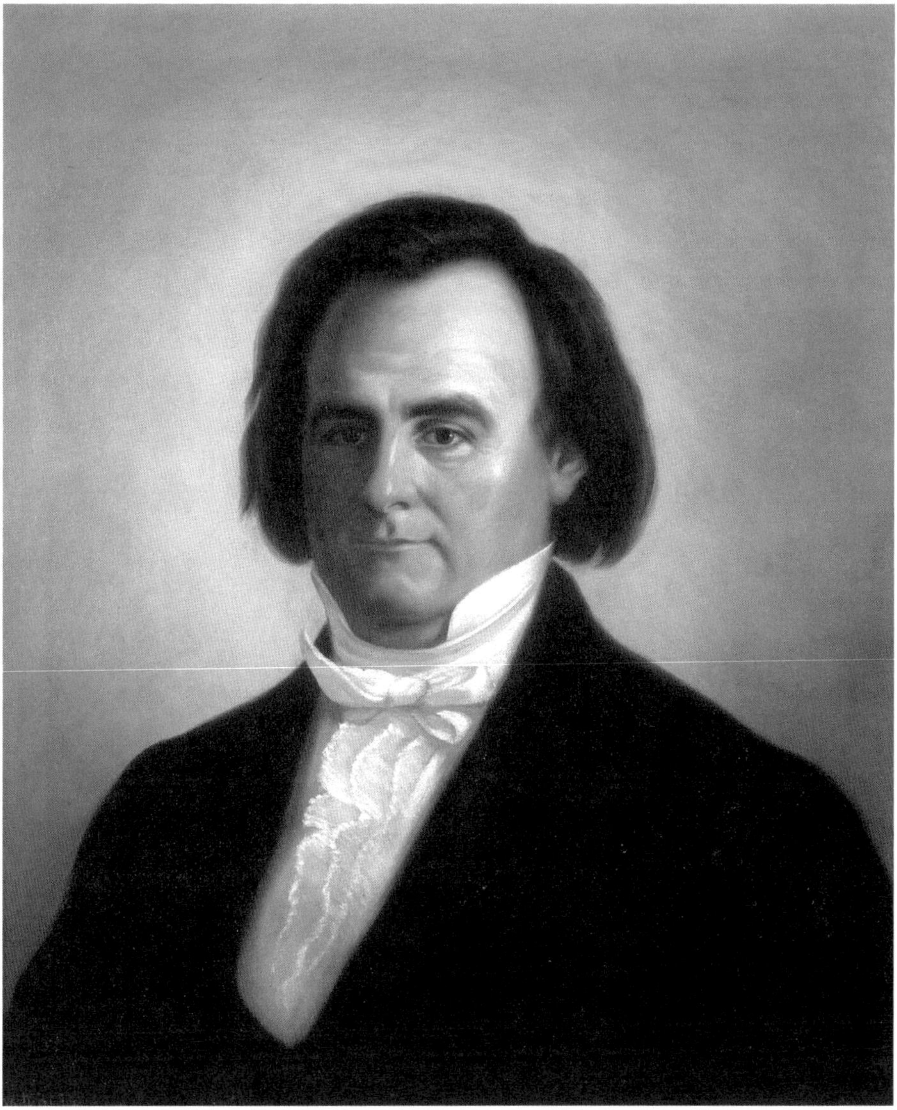

Charles A. Wickliffe (1788–1869). *Courtesy of the Kentucky Historical Society.*

General Ambrose E. Burnside declared martial law, claiming that it was necessary to keep disloyal Kentuckians from voting. Union Democrat Thomas Bramlette won in a landside.

"But, of course, the outcome was not a good gauge of Kentucky's preference," said Duane Bolin, a Murray State University historian and author. He quoted *A New History of Kentucky*: "No disloyal person was to be allowed to vote, and an estimated third of potential voters were kept from the polls."

Wickliffe's home, built in the early 1800s, is preserved in Bardstown, the Nelson County seat. The historical marker says Wickland "is known as the home of 3 governors: the builder, gov. of Ky., 1839–40; his son, Robert C. Wickliffe, gov. of Louisiana, 1856–60; and his grandson, J.C.W. Beckham, gov. of Ky., 1900–07."

Wickliffe was elected lieutenant governor in 1836. He finished the term of Governor James Clark, who died.

Shortly after the Civil War began in 1861, Wickliffe was elected to Congress again, as a Unionist. But he ultimately joined the Southern-sympathizing Peace Democrats.

The Collins history book praises Wickliffe for mustering "the moral and physical courage, in the teeth of bayonets and the threat of arrest, to make the race…for governor." But Peace Democrat Wickliffe was also a battler. A combat veteran of the War of 1812, he fought off an assassination attempt while he was postmaster general.

In 1843, an assailant stuck Wickliffe "twice in the breast with a clasp knife," according to *History of Kentucky*. "The young man was found to be insane, and sent to an asylum." Wickliffe died in 1869 at age eighty-one.

"McCreary's Bird"

James B. McCreary was a two-time governor of Kentucky. He wasn't a two-timer, though he is buried in Richmond Cemetery with his wife and Polly, his "longtime companion."

Polly was McCreary's pet bird, apparently a parrot. "One of McCreary's enemies said the bird was so dear to him because it was the only creature from whom he would take advice," Bryant said. "If the governor asked the bird if someone should be trusted in politics, it would make a gesture with its head in affirmative or negative response. Another story was that the bird advised McCreary on the character of someone by calling out 'rascal.'"

A Democrat, McCreary was governor from 1875 to 1879 and again from 1911 to 1915. At the time he was first elected, the thirty-seven-year-old McCreary was Kentucky's youngest governor. In 1901, that distinction passed to J.C.W. Beckham, the lieutenant governor who became governor at age thirty after Governor William Goebel was assassinated. McCreary is still Kentucky's oldest governor, beginning his second term at age seventy-three.

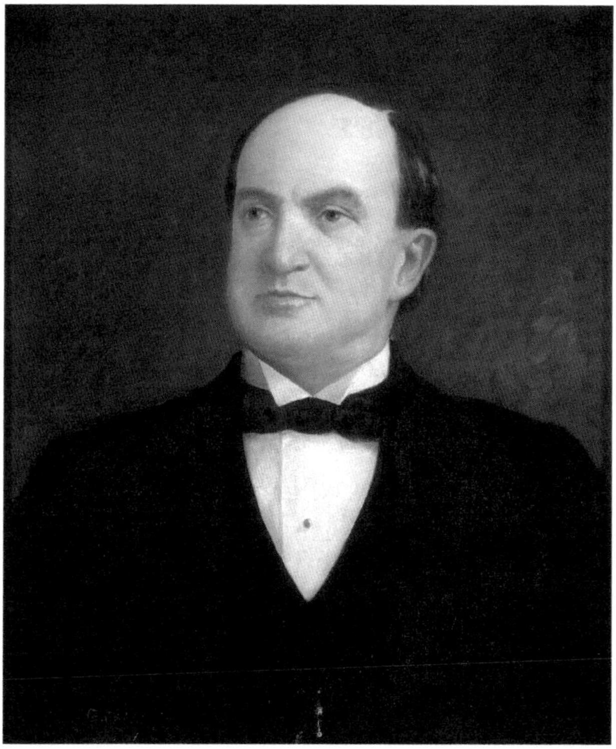

James B. McCreary (1838–1918). *Courtesy of the Kentucky Historical Society.*

Born near Richmond, the Madison County seat, in 1838, McCreary became a lawyer before riding off to the Civil War in Rebel gray. He soldiered under General John Hunt Morgan, the famous Confederate cavalry commander from Lexington, and made lieutenant colonel.

Before he was governor, McCreary was Speaker of the Kentucky House of Representatives. In between his terms as Bluegrass State chief executive, the ex-Rebel served in the U.S. House and Senate.

McCreary's enemies often accused him of straddling the fence. His detractors dubbed him "Bothsides" and "Oily Jeems" because he was "so slippery on issues," explains *A New History of Kentucky*. "According to a popular story of the time," the authors added, "McCreary had once been observing black sheep in a field, and someone remarked on their color: 'Well, they do appear to be black on this side at least,' he responded." Harrison and Klotter also quoted McCreary on banning booze: "If the people of Kentucky are for prohibition, I'm for it. If the people of Kentucky are against prohibition, I'm against prohibition."

Bryant doubts that Polly was McCreary's avian aide. Evidently, she was just a feathered friend.

"The most likely story is the least interesting one," he said. "The bird was a special gift and became a longtime companion of McCreary. He thought so much of the bird that it was felt the two should not be parted in death."

McCreary, for whom McCreary County is named, died in 1918. His memorial, a rough-hewn sandstone boulder, identifies him as a two-time governor and a "soldier-statesman-patriot."

Polly perished in 1920 and is buried under a tiny marker with the simple epitaph, "McCreary's Bird." "That, of course, could be interpreted different ways," Bryant suggested.

"Dr. Blackvomit"

Was Governor Luke P. Blackburn a bioterrorist?

Yankee Republicans charged that Blackburn, a physician, tried to spread deadly yellow fever epidemics in the North during the Civil War. "Yes, he did practice germ warfare," said Nancy Disher Baird, a Western Kentucky University librarian, historian and Blackburn biographer. "But he didn't kill anybody because he didn't know what really caused yellow fever."

The *Aedes aegypti* mosquito carries the disease. Nobody knew that until 1900, Baird added.

Meanwhile, the GOP-friendly *Cincinnati Gazette* ran a story shortly after the Democrats nominated Blackburn in 1879, claiming that a Dr. Blackburn was tried in Toronto in 1865 for violating Canada's neutrality by importing clothes from yellow fever victims into Canada. Allegedly, Confederate spies were to sneak back over the border with the thought to be deadly duds and distribute them in Northern cities, thereby spreading the malady.

In her book, *Luke Pryor Blackburn*, Baird said that details of the trial have been lost. But, she added, the *New York Times* reported that the doctor was acquitted.

Blackburn, born in Woodford County in 1816, grew up to become a doctor and an alleged authority on yellow fever. He moved south, where he battled the disease by quarantining patients.

He also rushed to Hickman in 1878 to help yellow fever patients there. Blackburn was hailed in Kentucky and the South as the "Hero of Hickman." When he ran for governor in 1879, he was cursed in the North as "Dr. Blackvomit" because yellow fever victims vomit blood.

The hero and bioterrorist labels applied to Blackburn are hard to reconcile, Baird admits. "Blackburn's humanitarian efforts before and after the war are incongruent with the charge of deliberate mass murder," she wrote. "But war does bring out the worst in human nature; perhaps the doctor believed

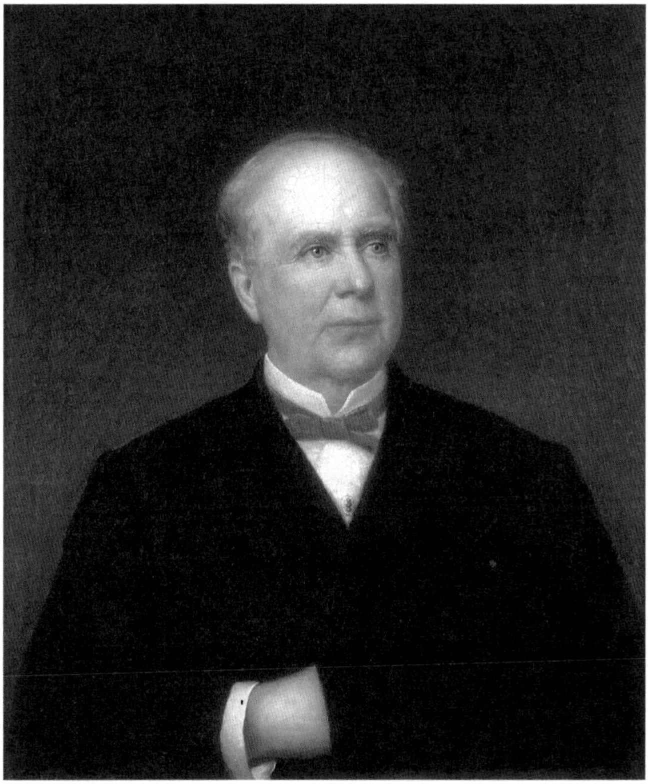

Luke P. Blackburn (1816–1887). *Courtesy of the Kentucky Historical Society.*

that he had the same right to use his skills and knowledge to slay the enemy as had any general."

Blackburn denied that he tried to practice germ warfare. He said the charge was "too preposterous for intelligent gentlemen to believe," Baird wrote.

Meanwhile, Editor Henry Watterson's staunchly Democratic *Louisville Courier-Journal* rushed to Blackburn's defense. In turn, Richard Smith, editor of the *Gazette*, hurled down the gauntlet.

"The Courier-Journal snarls and makes faces about the Blackburn business, but it dares not to say that Dr. Luke P. Blackburn, candidate for governor of Kentucky, is not the Luke P. Blackburn against whom the yellow-fever and small-pox charges were made," Baird wrote. Smith apparently tossed in the pox for extra measure.

Watterson matched innuendo with innuendo, according to Baird. He demanded to know if the Richard Smith who reportedly raped his niece, then set fire to her house and killed her to cover the crime was "the Richard Smith, proprietor of the Cincinnati Gazette, or is he some other Richard Smith?"

The *Philadelphia Press*, another Republican sheet, also blasted Blackburn. The *Press* published what it said were true accounts of witnesses to the doctor's misdeeds.

Watterson was predictably unimpressed. "The sworn testimony of Republican pimps, perjurers and murderers is not to be accepted by honest men," he replied in his paper, according to Baird.

In the August election, Blackburn beat Republican Walter Evans of Hopkinsville by about forty-three thousand votes. Governor Blackburn became famous for prison reform. The Blackburn Correctional Complex, a minimum security prison for men near Lexington, was named for the governor.

Blackburn died in 1887 at age seventy-one. Dubbed "the 'father' of prison reform in Kentucky," according to Baird, he was buried in the Frankfort Cemetery.

Blackburn favored rehabilitation over punishment. To ease prison overcrowding, he pardoned many inmates. In addition, he upgraded the Frankfort Penitentiary and pushed for construction of a new prison at Eddyville, the *Kentucky Encyclopedia* says. "He probably went into office as Kentucky's most popular governor and finished his term as our most unpopular, because of his pardons and his desire to spend taxpayers' money to improve conditions at Kentucky's penitentiaries," Baird said.

"Old Bol" Bore an Old Enemy to His Grave

Rebel General Simon Bolivar Buckner surrendered Fort Donelson but not his Kentucky hospitality. After he ran up the white flag, the Hart County native asked Yankee General Lew Wallace to breakfast. Twenty-three years later, Buckner agreed to serve as a pallbearer for General Ulysses S. Grant, to whom he relinquished Fort Donelson, near Dover, Tennessee.

Wallace, Buckner and Grant knew each other before the Civil War. Buckner and Grant were at West Point at the same time and fought together in the Mexican-American War.

Buckner, born near Munfordville, the Hart County seat, in 1823, helped Grant when he resigned from the army in 1854. Grant ended up in New York, down on his luck and short of cash to pay for a hotel room.

He contacted Buckner, who was also in the city. "Buckner agreed to guarantee the bill until Grant's father could send him the money," said Buzz Bazar, who was a park ranger at Fort Donelson National Battlefield. "Grant didn't forget that."

Apparently, they didn't meet again until February 16, 1862, when Buckner gave up Fort Donelson to his old army buddy following a bloody battle.

The earthen fort, a cannon-bristling bastion on the Cumberland River, is preserved in the park. So are Confederate outer trenches and the two-story, wooden Dover Hotel, where Buckner officially capitulated to Grant.

Buckner recalled that after the surrender formalities, Grant pulled him aside and offered him money. Buckner politely refused.

Buckner was sent to Fort Warren, Massachusetts, as a prisoner of war. "Grant wrote Buckner a letter of introduction so he might be afforded better treatment when he got there," Bazar said.

Released through a prisoner exchange, Buckner got back into Rebel gray. He fought in several more battles.

Before Grant arrived to accept Buckner's surrender, Wallace broke bread with Buckner and his staff. Apparently, Wallace, from Indiana, also knew Buckner from the Mexican-American War.

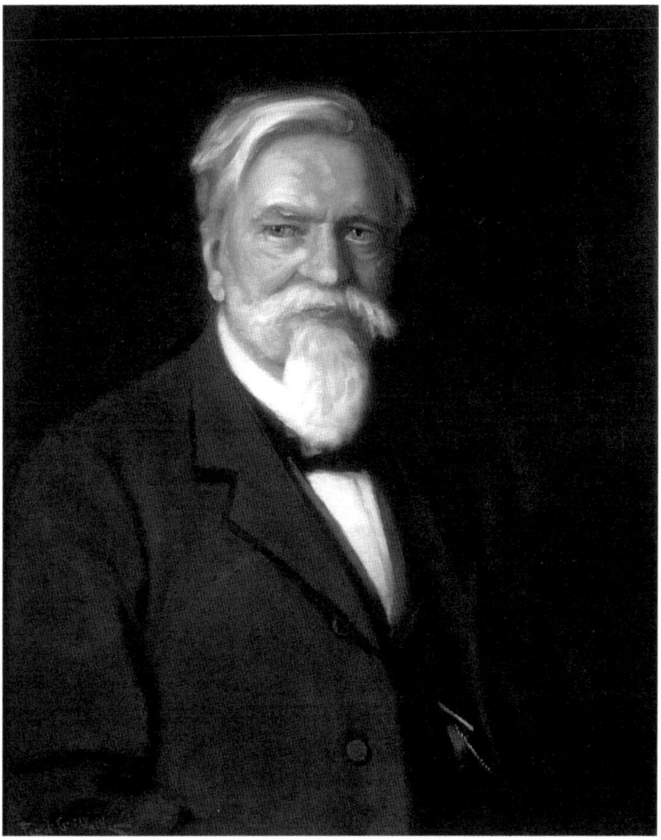

Simon Buckner (1823–1914). *Courtesy of the Kentucky Historical Society.*

"He met me with politeness and dignity," Wallace wrote in *Battles and Leaders of the Civil War*. "Turning to the officers at the table, he remarked: 'General Wallace, it is not necessary to introduce you to these gentlemen; you are acquainted with them all.'"

Wallace shook hands with the Rebel brass. "I was then invited to breakfast, which consisted of corn bread and coffee, the best the gallant officer had in his kitchen," added Wallace, author of *Ben Hur*. "We sat at the table about an hour and a half, when General Grant arrived and took temporary possession of the tavern as his headquarters."

Grant was elected president in 1868 and served two terms. Nicknamed "Old Bol," Buckner was governor of Kentucky from 1887 to 1891. He was a Democrat.

In 1885, Buckner and his second wife, Delia, were honeymooning in Saratoga, New York. They decided to visit Grant, who was dying of throat cancer at nearby Mount McGregor, New York.

Buckner tried to cheer Grant, who was unable to speak. He reminded the general of a badly wounded officer they knew from the Mexican War. Given up for dead, the man survived. In a handwritten note to Buckner, Grant said that he would not recover. Grant died about two weeks after Buckner's visit and was entombed in New York City. Buckner was one of four pallbearers.

A *New York Times* reporter asked the ex–Rebel general how he felt about helping lay to rest the Yankees' greatest general. Buckner, according to the scribe, stiffly refused a response, "except to say that General Grant had a great heart."

Buckner died in 1914. He was ninety.

"BILLY O'B"

William O'Connell Bradley of Lancaster, Kentucky's first Republican governor, was a liberal, at least by Bluegrass State standards.

"To his credit, Bradley supported greater black rights at a time when few [whites] did," said Klotter, state historian of Kentucky. "In a book devoted to the lives of African Americans in Kentucky and published in his lifetime, he is the only white person included, a testament to his standing in the black community."

Elected in 1895, Bradley was also "the father of the Republican party in Kentucky," according to M.H. Thatcher, Bradley's biographer. Before Bradley, Democrats held the governor's office for thirty-six years.

Senator Mitch McConnell is commonly credited with making the Republicans a force in current Kentucky politics. In his day, Bradley

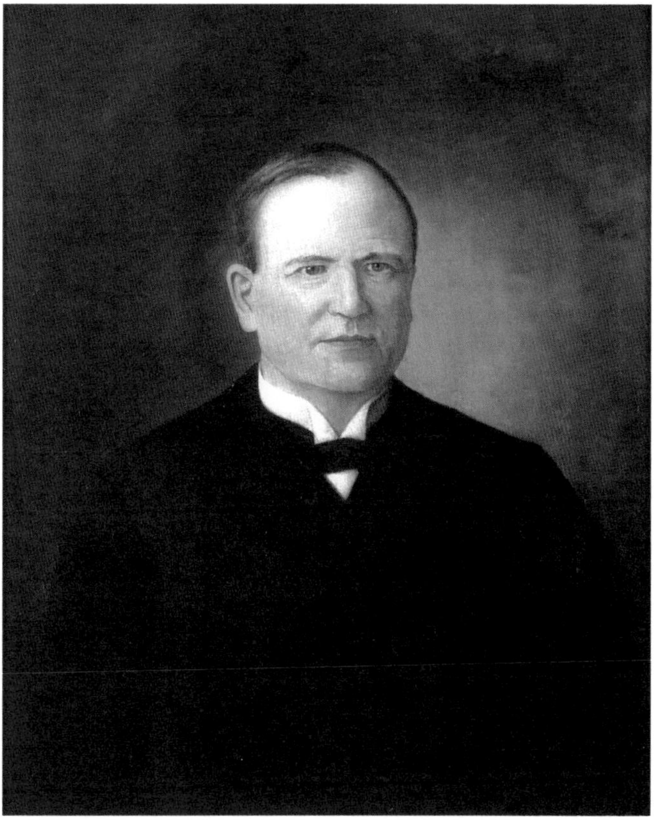

William O. Bradley (1847–1914). *Courtesy of the Kentucky Historical Society.*

was "the leading Republican in the state," according to the *Kentucky Encyclopedia*. "[Bradley]…certainly took a struggling party and gave it the voice and the strength to win elections," said Klotter, a history professor at Georgetown College.

Bradley was born in 1847 near Lancaster, the Garrard County seat. Pro-Union in the Civil War like most Garrard Countians, young William ran away to join the Yankee army at age fourteen. Fetched home by his father, the future governor took up the study of law in Lancaster. He was licensed as an attorney at age eighteen.

In 1870, voters elected Bradley county attorney. Thereafter, he spent "more than forty years…on the firing line, fighting the battles of the Republican party," Thatcher wrote in his book *Stories and Speeches of William O. Bradley*.

Bradley was a famous wit and stump orator. "What made him more appealing was that even his enemies could not help liking him," said Klotter, also an author and history professor at Georgetown College.

Bradley's foes ruled the political roost in post–Civil War Kentucky. The Bluegrass State was part of the Democratic "Solid South."

Bradley made his first run for governor in 1887. His Democratic opponent was the popular Simon Bolivar Buckner, an ex-Rebel general.

"Old Bol" bested "Billy O'B." But Bradley did better than expected, and he enjoyed strong backing from African Americans.

The Republicans went with Bradley again in 1895. Once more, he campaigned for black votes, prompting the divided and desperate Democrats to pander to white prejudice more than usual. Bradley won anyway.

In 1908, the state legislature elected him to the U.S. Senate. But he died in 1914 shortly before his term ended. Nonetheless, according to Thatcher, Bradley lived long enough to see "his planting and sowing in the political field grow unto golden harvest."

THE GOVERNOR WHO BEAT A MURDER RAP BEFORE HE WAS MURDERED

William Goebel went down in history as Kentucky's martyred governor. But he had blood on his hands, too. He beat a murder rap.

Few states have elected a governor who killed a political foe in a shootout. "But Kentucky had a reputation for violence," Bolin said. "Kentucky history is an odd paradox of piety versus passion."

Goebel, a Covington Democrat, became governor in 1900 after the most controversial election in Bluegrass State history. The vote was close and hotly disputed. Republicans charged that Goebel stole the office and insisted that their man, William S. Taylor, was governor.

Just when it looked like civil war between Democrats and Republicans might erupt in Frankfort, an unknown assassin shot Goebel on January 30, 1900. He died on February 3.

Almost five years earlier, Goebel had been the triggerman in the fatal shooting of John L. Sanford, cashier at Farmers and Traders Bank in Covington. Goebel went free after the only two witnesses to the shooting—one was Kentucky's attorney general—could not agree on who fired first.

Before he became governor, the Pennsylvania-born Goebel was a state senator, lawyer and newspaper owner in Covington. The bad blood between Goebel and Sanford, who was also a Democrat, boiled over when the senator called the banker "Col. John Gon-h-hea Sanford" in his newspaper.

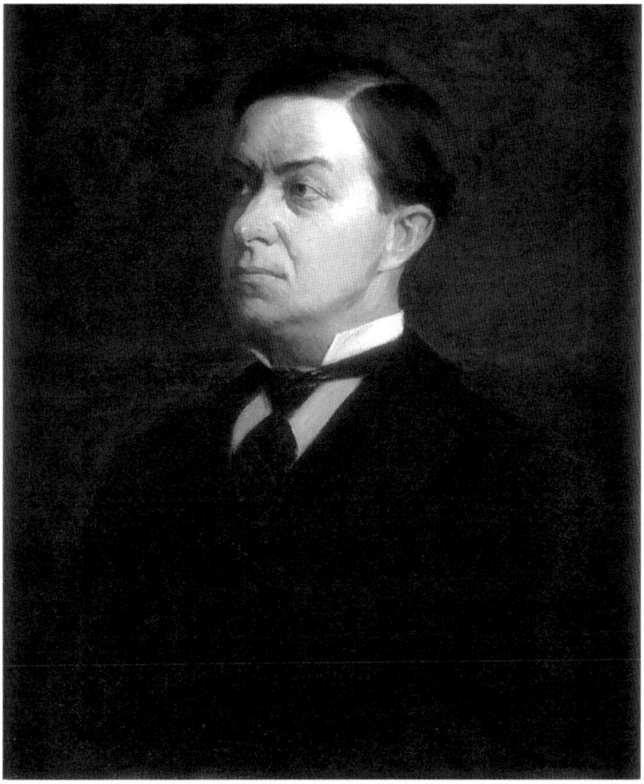

William J. Goebel (1856–1900). *Courtesy of the Kentucky Historical Society.*

The showdown came on April 11, 1895, when Sanford confronted Goebel in the doorway of Covington's First National Bank. They pulled pistols from their pockets and fired almost simultaneously at point-blank range. The senator fatally wounded Sanford in the forehead, according to *Famous Kentucky Tragedies and Trials* by L.F. Johnson.

Miraculously, Goebel was unscathed. Sanford's bullet holed the senator's "coat in front and passed across his left hip ranging downward, entered his trousers and passed through cutting the flap of his cutaway coat and splitting the left flap at the hip," Johnson wrote. "The skin was not broken."

Goebel was charged with killing Sanford, and a judge convened a pretrial hearing. Attorney General W.J. Hendricks, who went with Goebel to the bank, said he didn't "know who shot first, the shots were so close together," according to Johnson's book.

First National Bank President Frank P. Helm was so close to the gunplay that he suffered powder burns on his face. But Helm confessed that he could "not say positively which fired first."

The judge let Goebel go, citing insufficient evidence to convict the senator. Later, a grand jury declined to indict Goebel. Sanford's widow also sued Goebel for $10,000, "but the jury refused to find anything for the plaintiff," Johnson wrote.

Goebel stayed in the state senate and became speaker pro tempore. Writing in *The Kentucky Encyclopedia*, Harrison notes that Goebel went to his grave "a complex, ambitious person...denounced by some as a ruthless, heartless demagogue and hailed by others as a compassionate, dedicated reformer."

"The Terrible Turk from Madisonville"

Ernie Fletcher wasn't the only governor who was elected in a landslide but ended up in hot water with the voters. "At least a mob didn't attack the governor's mansion," said John Robertson. "That happened to Governor Ruby Laffoon."

A Madisonville Democrat, Laffoon proposed a penny sales tax during the Depression. He was scorned as "the Terrible Turk from Madisonville."

Fletcher, a Lexington Republican, was elected in 2003 and lost in a blowout four years later. He was sunk by a scandal over alleged abuses in the state's hiring system. Fletcher was indicted but not tried.

State revenues were plummeting when Laffoon took office in 1931. "He wanted to balance the budget," Robertson said.

To help refill state coffers, Laffoon urged the General Assembly to approve the sales tax in 1932. "This will be the most popular law passed this session," he predicted.

Poor Kentuckians, many of them jobless, denounced the tax. Merchants also opposed it; thousands of them rallied against the tax in Frankfort, the state capital, on March 3, 1932.

About one hundred men and women did more than verbally abuse Laffoon's levy. They raided the governor's mansion, scaring the staff, trashing the floors and slightly damaging some furnishings, according to the Associated Press.

Nobody got hurt, the wire service reported. Laffoon was in the capitol building; his wife and two daughters also were away. The governor's two grandchildren, ages two and a half and eleven, were home "but were not molested," the AP said.

Laffoon condemned the attack as "a disgrace and an outrage." But he decided not to press charges and "preferred to let the incident drop," the AP explained.

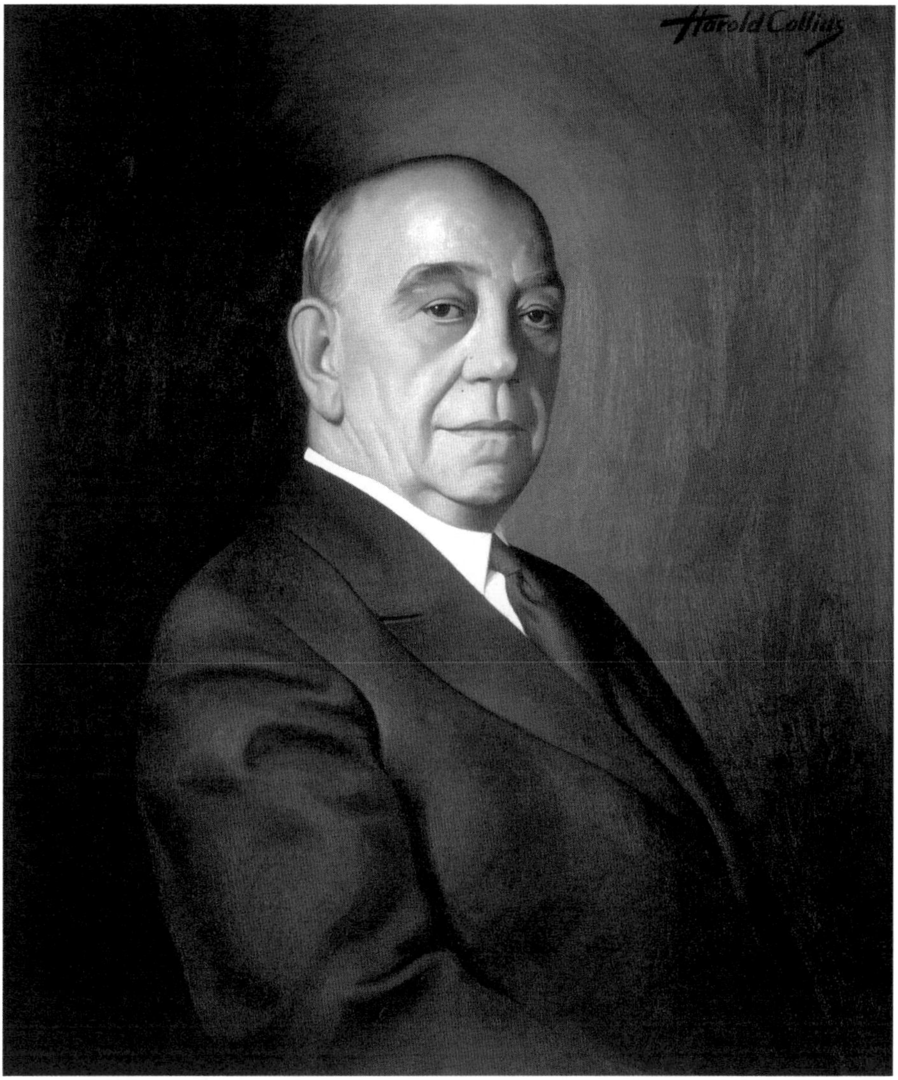

Ruby Laffoon (1869–1941). *Courtesy of the Kentucky Historical Society.*

The merchants also disavowed the assault. They promised it wasn't "part of their program of protest." Even so, many in the mob sported "badges such as were worn to identify members of the protesting delegation," said doorman Douglas Majors.

The mob shoved past Majors. "This is not the governor's house; it belongs to us because we paid the taxes for it," the intruders announced, according to the AP.

Majors said that many of the marauders appeared to be drunk. They demanded "coffee but were told there was none prepared."

According to Majors, the mob spent an hour in the mansion. One man purportedly packed a pistol but didn't pull it, the AP reported.

Majors told the AP that the invaders "ate sandwiches they brought with them, played the piano and inspected most of the rooms on the ground floor." They did not go upstairs, he added.

Laffoon claimed that the uninvited guests "carelessly disposed of cigarette butts, burning holes in the carpet and searing furniture." He also said they stole several light bulbs.

The Democratic-majority legislature refused to approve the sales tax in 1932 and again in 1933. According to *A New History of Kentucky*, Laffoon was "a sad figure by term's end [and]...lived in the mansion under guard to keep another mob away." He "went into a sanatorium to be treated for exhaustion, and then had to have surgery for appendicitis." The authors added, "In 1935 Laffoon left an office that had overwhelmed him."

Laffoon died in 1941. He is buried in Madisonville, the Hopkins County seat, where he was born in 1869. A state historical marker about Laffoon on the courthouse lawn is silent about the assault on the governor's mansion and the Terrible Turk's troubled tenure.

Local Democrats host an annual Ruby Laffoon dinner in Madisonville.

CHAPTER THREE

Kentuckians in the National Capital (and Their Relations)

"An Infernal Old Jackass"

No son of Kentucky is more famous or more revered than Abraham Lincoln. His 1809 birthplace near Hodgenville, the Larue County seat, is a national shrine. Lincoln's statue stands tall in the capitol rotunda in Frankfort.

Yet no president was more unpopular in Kentucky than Lincoln, who earned less than 1 percent of the Bluegrass State's vote when he won the White House in 1860. He managed only 30.2 percent in 1864.

The *Kentucky Statesman*, a Lexington newspaper, said that Lincoln was scared to campaign in his native state, according to *Lincoln and the Bluegrass: Slavery and Civil War in Kentucky* by William H. Townsend. "Lincoln told a correspondent that he had received an invitation to come to Kentucky, but declined because he thought it was a mere trap of the Kentuckians to catch him, tar and feather him, and set him on fire to make a torch-light procession of him," the paper reported.

The *Statesman* was stretching the truth. Presidential candidates mostly stayed home in Lincoln's day. Additionally, Lincoln and the Republicans were antislavery. They knew their man had no chance to carry Kentucky or any other slave state.

Even so, the national celebration of Lincoln's 200th birthday started in Kentucky with a February 12, 2008 program at the Abraham Lincoln Birthplace National Historic Site.

Most Kentuckians know that February 12 is Lincoln's birthday, but they are probably unaware how unloved Lincoln was in Kentucky. After all, Lincoln went down in history as one of America's greatest presidents.

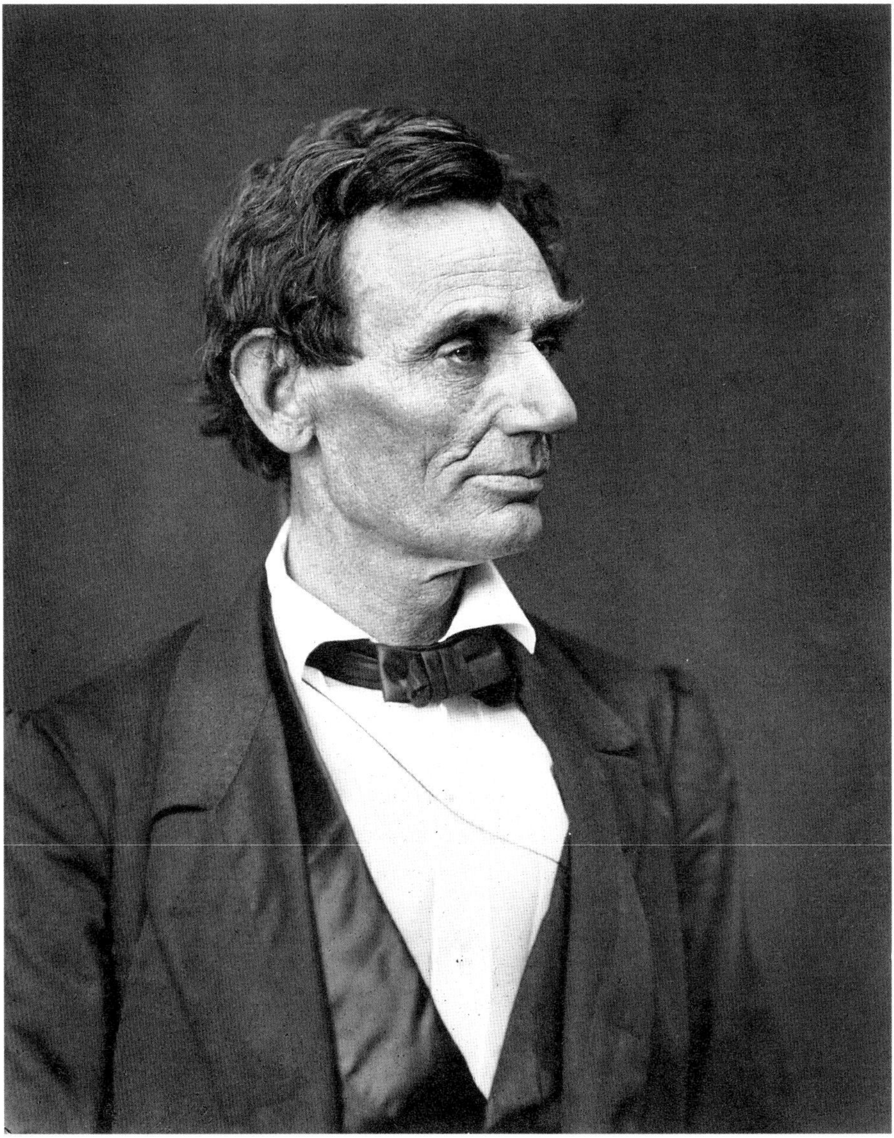

Abraham Lincoln (1809–1865). *Courtesy of the Kentucky Historical Society.*

But no president lost an election in Kentucky by a wider margin than Lincoln did in 1860. Tennessean John Bell, candidate of the Constitutional Union Party, earned Kentucky's dozen electoral votes with 66,051 ballots to 53,143 for John C. Breckinridge of Lexington, the Southern Democrat, according to *Presidential Politics in Kentucky 1824–1948* by Jasper B. Shannon and

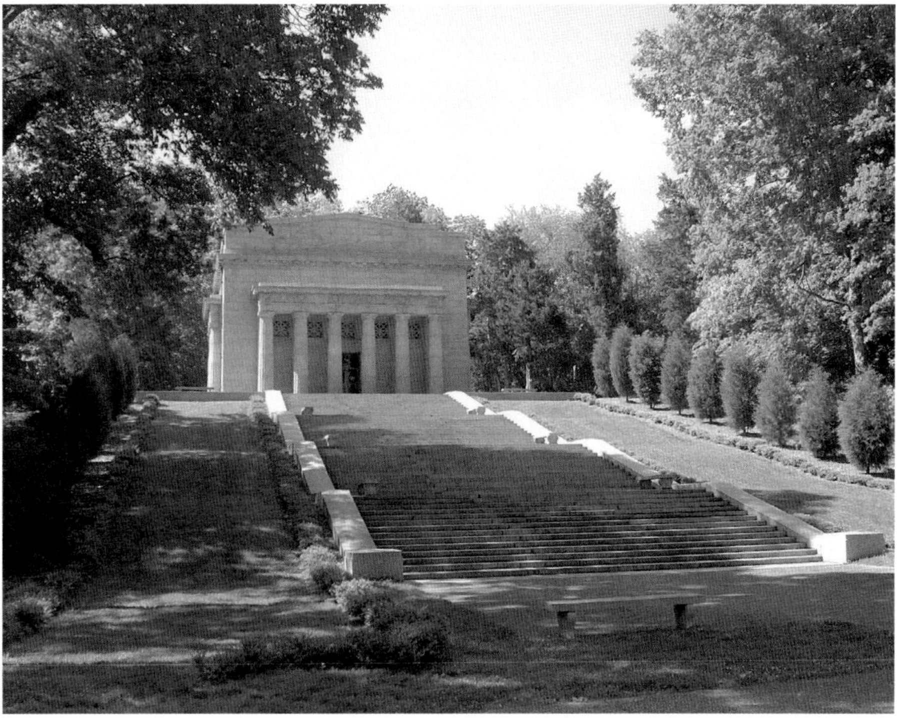

Abraham Lincoln Birthplace National Historic Site in Hodgenville, Kentucky.

Ruth McQuown. Northern Democrat Stephen A. Douglas of Illinois received 25,638 votes in Kentucky. Lincoln's total was 1,364, the authors added.

Even his home county spurned him. (Lincoln was actually born in southern Hardin County, from which Larue County was created in 1843.) Douglas carried Larue County, where Lincoln collected just three votes, Shannon and McQuown reported.

First Lady Mary Todd Lincoln was from Lexington, the Fayette County seat. Bell took the county, which furnished Lincoln only five votes, according to *Presidential Politics in Kentucky*.

According to Townsend, the pro-Breckinridge and pro-Southern *Statesman* editorialized that "no intelligent man of the South will fail to deprecate the election of Lincoln and therein the success of the Republican party as the most serious and lamentable calamity which could have befallen our Republic."

He also cited a letter from a young Lexingtonian who dubbed the president-elect

> *an infernal old Jackass. I should relish his groans and agonies if I could see him put to torture in hell or anywhere else. He has chosen to become the representative of the Republican Party and as such I should like to hang him.*

On his birthday in 1861, Lincoln tried to reassure the slave states in a speech he gave in Cincinnati, where he stopped en route to Washington by train. John Jeffrey of Lexington heard Lincoln and was not impressed.

Townsend quoted Jeffrey's letter to his brother back home:

> *Old Abe…looks, talks, & acts just as you may have seen some long, slab sided flat boat "Capting," who had sold his "prodooce" at Memphis & invested 12$ at a slop shop tailor's in rigging himself out for Sunday. He is a disgrace as the headboss of any civilized nation.*

Lincoln's aides, fearing he might be murdered by Southern sympathizers in Baltimore, persuaded the president to slip into Washington via night train from Harrisburg, Pennsylvania. The *Louisville Daily Courier*, Kentucky's leading secessionist paper, called the president-elect a coward.

"Lincoln said in Philadelphia before Independence Hall that he would rather be assassinated than abandon the principles of the Declaration of Independence," Townsend quoted the paper.

> *But within a week he ran from the first whisperings of danger as fleetly as ever a naked-legged Highlander pursued a deer upon Scotia's hills…No Kentucky-born man ever would have run all the way from Harrisburg to Washington, with but the ghost of an enemy in sight.*

Predictably, the *Statesman* gave Lincoln's inaugural address of March 4, 1861, a less than rave review, Townsend wrote. The paper claimed that Kentuckians disdained the president's remarks as

> *radical, sectional and abhorrent…Lincoln's silly speeches, his ill-timed jocularity and his pusillanimous evasion of responsibility and vulgar pettifoggery have no parallel in history, save the crazy capers of* [Roman Emperor] *Caligula, or in the effeminate buffoonery of Henry of Valois* [King Henry III of France].

Soon afterward, the *Courier* published a letter—omitting the signature—purportedly from "a prominent member of Congress," Townsend wrote. He quoted from the letter, which echoed the *Courier*'s editorial slant:

> *Lincoln is a cross between a sand-hill crane and an Andalusian Jackass. He is, by all odds, the weakest man who has ever been elected...I was sent for by him. I speak what I know.*
>
> *He is vain, weak, puerile, hypocritical, without manners, without social grace, and as he talks to you, punches his fists under your ribs. He swears equal to Uncle Toby* [a character in *Tristram Shandy*], *and in every particular, morally and mentally, I have lost all respect for him...He is surrounded by a set of toad-eaters and bottle-throwers.*

The Civil War began on April 12, 1861, when the Confederates fired on Fort Sumter, in Charleston, South Carolina. The *Statesman* charged that Lincoln, "the miserable imbecile that now disgraces the Presidential chair," started the war, Townsend wrote.

After a brief period of neutrality in 1861, Kentucky forthrightly declared for the Union. Perhaps three times more Kentuckians donned Yankee blue than put on Rebel gray.

But in Kentucky, loyalty to the Union usually did not mean loyalty to Lincoln. Most Kentuckians, even ardent Unionists, were quick to make the distinction.

Almost all white Kentuckians hated Lincoln's Emancipation Proclamation, which put slavery on the road to extinction. They also fumed at the president's policy of enlisting ex-slaves in the Union army.

When Lincoln ran for reelection in 1864, it was obvious he would lose Kentucky again. "I am opposed to your election, and regard a change of policy as essential to the salvation of Kentucky," Lowell H. Harrison quoted Governor Thomas Bramlette, a Union Democrat, in *The Civil War in Kentucky*. Most Kentuckians agreed with their chief executive.

The *Louisville Daily Journal*, which had been the state's premier Union paper, denounced Lincoln. "Undoubtedly President Lincoln, on account of his position, is the chief tyrant of the country...," Robert Emmett McDowell quoted the newspaper in *City of Conflict: Louisville in the Civil War 1861–1865*.

Lincoln won a second term in a landslide. But Democrat George B. McClellan, a Union general, won the Bluegrass State in a blowout. Kentucky gave Lincoln "the lowest vote [he]...received in any of the 25 states which participated in the balloting in 1864," according to *Presidential Politics in Kentucky*. The authors added, "Notwithstanding their opposition to secession, the voters of the state indicated violent antagonism to the Republican leader, for he received less than one third of the total vote cast."

The president improved his score from 1860, when "he carried not a single county," Shannon and McQuown reported. In 1864, running on the Union ticket, not as a Republican, he carried 25 of 101 counties that posted returns. Nonetheless, McClellan outpolled Lincoln 64,301 to 27,787, according to *Presidential Politics in Kentucky*.

Lincoln became popular in Kentucky after he was assassinated. "A great transformation seems almost mysteriously to have swept over the people when the word came that Lincoln was dead," Coulter wrote in *The Civil War and Readjustment in Kentucky*. "From their customary attitude of condemnation and vilification, they now turned to honoring and praising. They speedily forgot their past four years' opposition to the President, who now lay dead, and they have never sought to recall it."

McDowell wrote that Bramlette issued a proclamation on April 17, 1865, three days after the president was shot and two days after he died. The proclamation called on Kentuckians "to pay homage to the national grief" over the loss of the president. "Let every church bell throughout the Commonwealth be tolled; on that day let every business be suspended, all business houses closed, and the public offices closed and draped in mourning," the proclamation urged.

Townsend wrote that "in Lexington the demonstration of grief was extensive and sincere." Nonetheless, he cited the *National Unionist*, a pro-Union Lexington paper, which reported:

> *We are sorry to have to record the fact that there were several large business houses of some of our citizens upon which there was no evidence, in the way of mourning emblems, of any sorrow at the death of the Chief Executive of the Nation...And we suppose that they really felt no sorrow.*

"STOP YOUR NONSENSE AND DRINK YOUR WHISKEY!"

When General Zachary Taylor of Jefferson County came home a hero from the Mexican-American War, the Whig Party wanted to run him for president.

A Whig bigwig told Taylor that the nomination was his for the asking. The old soldier didn't waste words on a reply. "Stop your nonsense and drink your whiskey!" he exclaimed, according to Paul F. Boller's book *Presidential Anecdotes*.

Dubbed "Old Rough and Ready" by his troops who idolized him, Taylor changed his mind. He was elected in 1848 but died suddenly in office in 1850. He was sixty-five.

Though Taylor was living in Louisiana when he was elected president, he grew up in Jefferson County, where he was buried. Taylor's tomb is the best-known gravesite in Zachary Taylor National Cemetery in Louisville. The 16.5-acre military burial ground is at 4701 Brownsboro Road. "A lot of people probably didn't know our twelfth president was buried in Louisville until there was all that business about exhuming his body in 1991 to see if he had been murdered," said Gary Peak, assistant director of the Kentucky National Cemetery Complex.

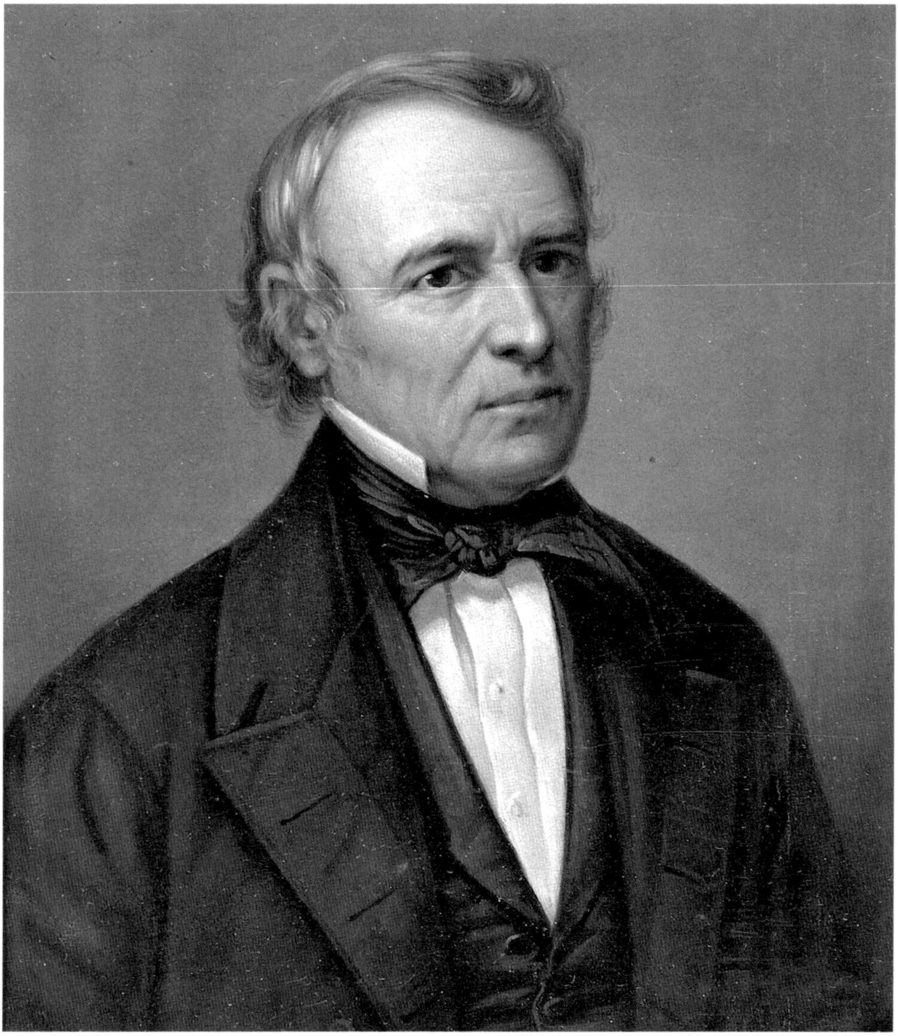

Zachary Taylor (1784–1850). *Courtesy of the Kentucky Historical Society.*

For the record, Taylor died of natural causes.

The president and his wife, Margaret Smith Taylor, are interred in a stone mausoleum that the federal government built for the Taylors in 1926. The Taylors were moved from an old family vault, which is nearby.

The presidential crypt is shadowed by a thirty-five-foot shaft topped by a marble statue of Taylor in a general's uniform. The president's reputed last words are chiseled on the monument's base: "I have endeavored to do my duty, I am ready to die."

The State of Kentucky erected the monument in 1883, thirty-five years after naming Taylor County for the soldier-president. Two other states claim Taylor as a presidential son: Virginia, where he was born in 1784, and Louisiana, where he also lived.

But Taylor considered Kentucky his official home, according to the *Kentucky Encyclopedia*. Lewis and Richard Collins's old *History of Kentucky* explained that Taylor "was brought by his parents to this State when only nine months old, and received his first impressions of the world amid the hearty hunters, the tall forests and romantic scenery of the dark and bloody ground."

In 1785, Taylor's father, Colonel Richard Taylor, a Revolutionary War veteran, migrated to Kentucky, settling on a farm he called Springfield. Son Zachary opted for a military career.

By the time the Mexican-American War broke out, Taylor was a veteran army man. He had soldiered in the War of 1812 and the Seminole Wars.

He became a national hero after beating the Mexican army in the bloody battle of Buena Vista, Mexico, in 1847. Taylor's troops reportedly were outnumbered about four to one. "Calm, collected, and resolved, he rose superior to the danger of his situation, and wrested victory from defeat," the Collins history book relates. "It is admitted by all who were present, that no man but General Taylor could have won the victory of Buena Vista."

A hard fighter on the battlefield, Taylor hated parade-ground spit and polish. His statue to the contrary, Taylor seldom wore a uniform in the Mexican-American War. He preferred a battered straw hat and plain civilian clothes. One officer said that "Old Rough and Ready" looked less like a general and "more like a farmer going to market with eggs to sell," according to *Presidential Anecdotes*.

Many northern Whigs opposed the Mexican-American War. They claimed that President James K. Polk, a southern slave-owning Democrat, provoked the war to grab Mexican territory, which he could turn into more slave states.

Though Taylor was the war's top general, the Whig brass opted for practical politics over principle. They figured he would be a shoo-in for

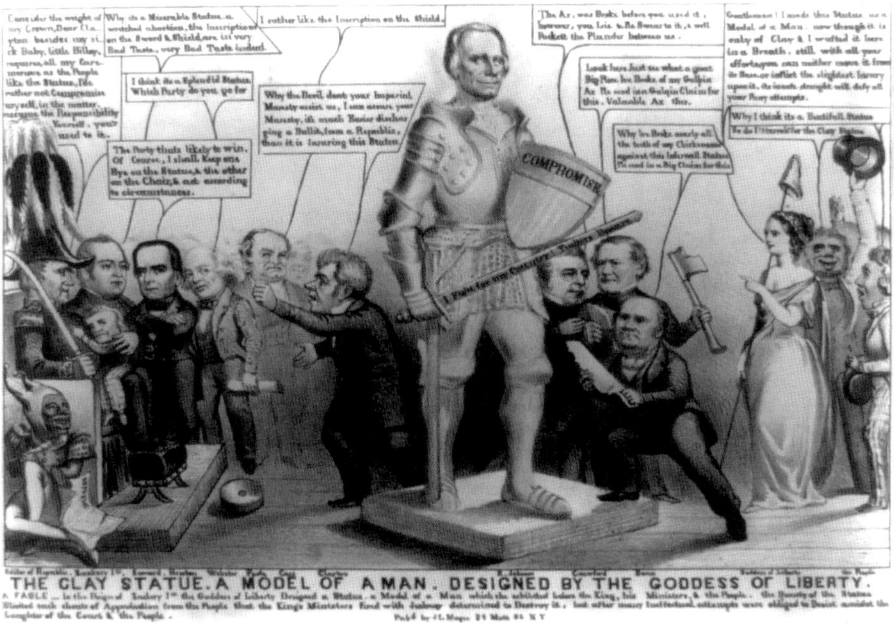

The artist lionizes Kentucky senator Henry Clay, author of the Compromise of 1850, and slams his political foes and critics of the compromise, particularly those in the Taylor administration. The text in the lower margin reads: "A Fable—In the Reign of Zackery 1st the Goddess of Liberty Designed a Statue, a Model of a Man which she exhibited before the King, his Ministers, & the People. John L. Magee, 1850." *Courtesy of the Library of Congress.*

president in 1848. An admirer predicted that the general would win by "spontaneous combustion."

It took votes, but Taylor won.

Taylor, too, was a slave owner. He also wanted to see the country grow. But he angered the proslavery South by supporting the admission of California as a free state in 1850.

In Congress, debate over California and the expansion of slavery heated up in the summer of that fateful year. Taylor took a day off on July 4 to attend cornerstone-laying ceremonies at the new Washington Monument.

It was hot as blue blazes; Taylor sat hatless in the sun. After the long program, he returned to the White House and tried to cool off. The president reputedly gobbled a bowl of raw vegetables or fruit, washing it down with iced milk.

He collapsed into bed with severe cramps, diarrhea and a burning fever. Doctors tried a variety of remedies, including bloodletting. Taylor suffered for five more days before he died.

The president's body rested in peace in Louisville until 1991, when it seemed like a real-life Agatha Christie novel was played out in the national cemetery. Clara Rising, a Florida author writing a book about Taylor, suggested that he might have been poisoned. She wondered if "Old Rough and Ready's" proslavery enemies might have spiked whatever he ingested with deadly arsenic.

Rising convinced officials to exhume Taylor's body. Samples of the president's hair, fingernails, teeth and breastbone were dispatched to laboratories for examination by experts.

"The story got national—even international—coverage in the media," said Peak, who is based at Zachary Taylor Cemetery. "But the tests proved that President Taylor had definitely not died of arsenic poison."

The experts concluded that the president's doctors might have unwittingly killed him by employing cures worse than the complaint. Or whatever he ate or drank may have been fatally contaminated by bacteria.

Kentucky's Golden Ticket

Two Kentucky natives running as Democrats in the presidential election of 1896 nudged the Bluegrass State into the GOP column for the first time.

"As far as I know, it was the only time two Kentucky-born candidates ever ran together," Klotter said. "They caused the state to go Republican, too."

John M. Palmer and Simon Bolivar Buckner, ex–Civil War generals and former governors, teamed up as "Gold Democrats." They collected 5,108 votes in Kentucky, which probably would have gone to regular Democrat William Jennings Bryan.

Republican William McKinley carried Kentucky by a mere 281 votes.

Anyway, the 1896 presidential election proved that politics, indeed, makes strange bedfellows. Palmer was a Scott County native who moved to Illinois. He was a Yankee general in America's bloodiest conflict and a Republican governor afterward. Later, he switched to the Democrats.

Buckner, from Hart County, donned Rebel gray and earned general's stars. He was Kentucky's governor from 1887 to 1891.

Five years later, the Democrats nominated the populist-minded Bryan, a Nebraskan, for president. He wanted the government to mint more silver coins, thereby inflating the currency and enabling poor farmers and other debtors to pay bills with cheaper dollars. Bryan also denounced big business monopolies.

McKinley, Ohio's governor, was pro-business and he favored the gold standard. He appealed to many conservative Kentucky Democrats who believed that Bryan was a dangerous radical.

Henry Watterson, editor of the usually Democratic *Louisville Courier-Journal*, deserted the thirty-six-year-old Bryan. "When he found himself well in the saddle he began to rule despotically and to ride furiously," Watterson wrote in his memoirs, *Marse Henry: An Autobiography*. "A party leader more shortsighted could hardly be imagined."

Anti-Bryan Democrats bolted to the party's national convention in Chicago and started the National or "Gold" Democrats. There was talk of a Watterson nomination for president.

But in the end, the National Democrats tapped Palmer for president and Buckner for his running mate. "There was quite a strong sentiment for gold in Kentucky, especially in the older, conservative wing of the Democratic Party," Klotter said. "Some of these wayward Democrats would return to the party but others would not."

Watterson did but defended his right to criticize fellow Democrats. "Things have come to a hell of a pass," he declared, according to Harrison and Klotter, "when a man can't whip his own jackass."

Stonewall's "Worthy Successor"

Thomas Jonathan "Stonewall" Jackson's "worthy successor" was a Kentucky general better known as a politician. "You could say that John C. Breckinridge is one of those guys who get sort of slighted in military history," said John Trowbridge, former director of the Kentucky Military Museum in Frankfort, the Bluegrass State capital.

Breckinridge's victory at the Civil War battle of New Market, Virginia, invited comparison with the storied "Stonewall" Jackson, one of the Confederacy's great heroes. "Even so, the battle is most famous for the charge of the VMI [Virginia Military Institute] cadets," Trowbridge said.

The cadets get top billing at the New Market Battlefield State Historical Park, a National Historic Landmark. The three-hundred-acre Shenandoah Valley site includes a Hall of Valor Civil War Museum, which features "a unique moment in American history—when college boys, Cadets from VMI, helped win a victory for the Confederate Army."

Contemporaries congratulated the cadets and their commander, a pre–Civil War state legislator, congressman, vice president, U.S. senator and presidential hopeful from Lexington, Kentucky. Some of Breckinridge's

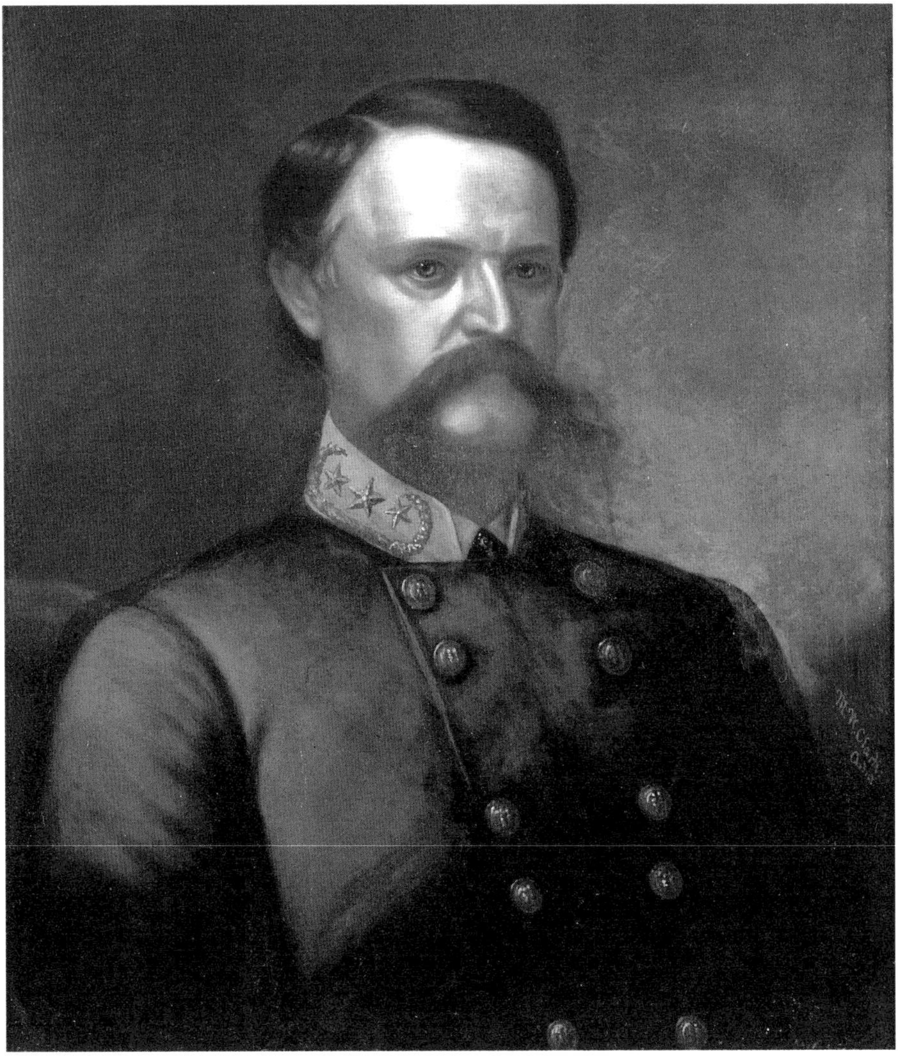

John C. Breckinridge (1821–1875). *Courtesy of the Kentucky Historical Society.*

New Market soldiers gave him a dress sword, which is displayed in the battlefield museum.

A grateful General Robert E. Lee telegraphed "the thanks of this army" to Breckinridge for winning at New Market on May 15, 1864, according to *Breckinridge: Statesman, Soldier, Symbol* by William C. Davis.

The author quoted the *Daily Dispatch* and the *Whig*, newspapers published in Richmond, the Confederate capital. "Gen. Breckinridge, in celerity of movement, has proved himself a worthy successor of Jackson," the *Dispatch* editorialized. "General Breckinridge seems to be following the example of our great Jackson," chimed the *Whig*.

Other parallels were cited. Breckinridge won at New Market on the first anniversary of Jackson's burial. A Virginian, West Point graduate and former VMI professor, Jackson was accidentally shot by his own troops at the Battle of Chancellorsville, Virginia, in May 1863.

"The comparison with Jackson was made complete by the fact that, in the battle [of New Market], Breckinridge rode a bay given to him by [Confederate General Benjamin Franklin] Cheatham, a horse which bore the same name as the mighty Stonewall's mount, 'Old Sorrel,'" Davis wrote. Jackson's horse was more often called "Little Sorrel."

Born in Lexington in 1821, Breckinridge became a lawyer, served in the Mexican-American War and entered politics. He was the star Democrat in Kentucky, a mostly Whig state.

In 1849, voters sent him to the state House of Representatives. Two years later, they elevated him to Congress, where he served until 1855. He was elected vice president in 1856.

In December 1859—long before the term was to begin—the Kentucky General Assembly elected him to the U.S. Senate, according to the *Kentucky Encyclopedia*. The next year, Breckinridge ran for president as a Southern Democrat. He finished second in the electoral college to Republican Abraham Lincoln, another Kentucky native, and second in the state to John Bell, the Constitutional Union party candidate. It was the only time Breckinridge lost an election, the *Kentucky Encyclopedia* reports.

Breckinridge led troops in several bloody battles in the western theater before being sent to Virginia. Davis called New Market "the most important secondary victory of the war in the East."

Breckinridge was named Confederate Secretary of War in 1865, the year America's bloodiest conflict ended in Southern defeat. He died in 1875 and was buried in Lexington Cemetery.

"Barkley Swept Here"

For years, that's what a small wooden sign bragged on the old Marvin College campus in Clinton, the Hickman County seat in deep western Kentucky.

The sign is gone. So is the little Methodist school whose most famous graduate was Alben Barkley, a vice president, Senate majority leader and congressman from nearby Paducah.

The sign was a spoof on the "Washington [as in George] slept here" claims from Revolutionary War–era homes and hostelries back East.

When he was a student at the college, Barkley landed a job as a janitor. "Mr. Homer Harpole put up the sign in the '40s or '50s," said John Kelley Ross Jr., a Clinton historian and the Hickman County Museum curator.

The president's home, which is empty, and the men's dormitory are all that remain of Marvin College, which closed in 1922. The three-story, 1910-vintage brick building is a private residence and a bed-and-breakfast inn.

A state historical society marker out front says that Barkley graduated from Marvin College in 1897 and "worked his way through by doing janitor work, giving rise to the phrase, 'Barkley swept here.'"

Barkley was born in 1877 on a farm close to Lowes in adjoining Graves County. His family moved to another farm near Clinton in 1891, according to the *Kentucky Encyclopedia*.

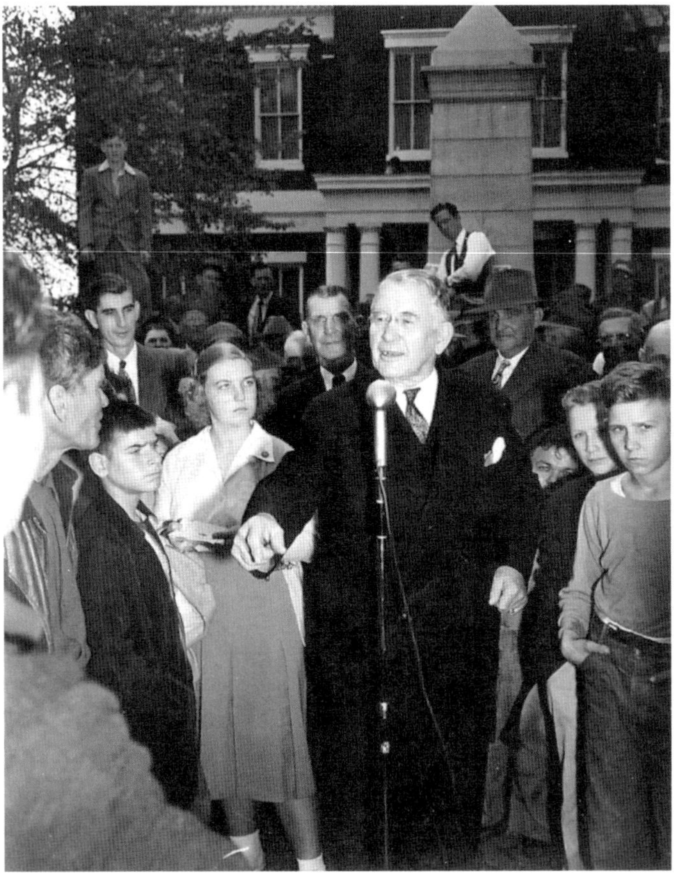

Alben W. Barkley (1877–1956).

Two of Barkley's teachers at Lowes encouraged him to go to college. They said he would be president some day.

Barkley preserved their prognostication in *That Reminds Me*, his autobiography. "Alas, for the predictions of these fine ladies, I did not quite make the presidency," wrote Barkley, dubbed "The Veep" for his vice-presidential tenure under President Harry Truman.

Barkley made it as a Marvin College janitor "after much maneuvering and negotiating" to convince the college president "Mr. J.C. Speight to bestow upon me the coveted janitor's job," he wrote.

Barkley added, "Years later I was pleased to award his son, Edmund Speight, one of my first Congressional appointments to Annapolis, and he made a fine record as a naval officer."

Barkley said that his custodial duties entailed sweeping, ringing the bell in the morning, dusting the benches, kindling fires, carrying water and "dozens of other chores."

Barkley ended up in Paducah. A Democrat, he served in the U.S. House of Representatives from 1913 to 1927 and in the U.S. Senate from 1927 to 1949. He was majority leader from 1937 to 1947 and minority leader from 1947 to 1949.

Barkley was vice president from 1949 to 1953. He was reelected to the Senate in 1954 and died in office in 1956.

After Harpole bought the college property, he tore down the main classroom building and used the bricks to build himself a house. "He put the wooden sign in his yard for fun," Ross said.

Ross isn't sure if a "Barkley Slept Here" sign would have been accurate. "I don't know if he lived with his parents or lived in the dorm," he said.

"Rumpsey Dumpsey"

It might not swing many votes in a modern political campaign, but "Rumpsey Dumpsey, Rumpsey Dumpsey, Colonel Johnson killed Tecumseh" was Richard Mentor Johnson's slogan when he ran for vice president in 1836.

The Kentucky Democrat was elected, but in 1837 and by the U.S. Senate because "no candidate received a majority of the electoral votes," according to the *Kentucky Encyclopedia*. Never before—or since—had a vice president been so chosen.

Johnson was from Great Crossing, near Georgetown, the Scott County seat. He never claimed that he ended the life of Tecumseh, the famous Shawnee chief, in the War of 1812. But he didn't stop anybody from saying he did.

Tecumseh fell in the 1813 Battle of the Thames in Canada. Who killed him is unknown. "Johnson may have been the one," Klotter said. "Others were said to have shot Tecumseh. So it is still a mystery."

Johnson's own recollections of the battle don't solve the riddle either. The colonel, who left his seat in Congress to command a regiment of Kentucky mounted riflemen, said only that he shot "an Indian chief."

Even so, he was dubbed "the Hero of the Thames," a bloody clash he barely survived. The colonel was "covered with wounds, twenty-five balls having been shot into him, his clothes, and his horse," according to Lewis and Richard Collins's old *History of Kentucky*. Johnson's bravery had "scarcely a parallel in the heroic annals of our country," the authors added.

Fought near Fairfield, Ontario, on October 5, 1813, the Battle of the Thames pitted about three thousand American troops against a force of about forty-five hundred British soldiers and their Native American allies, according to *A New History of Kentucky*.

"Johnson's regiment, divided into two sections, rode through the British regulars and routed them in a matter of minutes," Harrison and Klotter wrote. "When the half regiment led by Johnson encountered heavy fire from Indians who were concealed in the heavy growth of a swamp, Johnson dismounted his men to fight on foot."

Still astride his horse, Johnson summoned a twenty-man "Forlorn Hope" to draw the Indians' fire. "Fifteen were killed at once, and four were wounded," Harrison and Klotter wrote. Among the slain was sixty-four-year-old Lincoln County pioneer William Whitley.

Meanwhile Johnson, according to Collins,

> *was in the very midst and thickest of the fight, inspiring by his presence and courage the utmost confidence of his brave followers, and though perforated with balls, his bridle arm shattered, and bleeding profusely, he continued to fight until he encountered and slew an Indian chief who formed the rallying point of the savages. The chief was supposed to be the famous Tecumseh himself, upon whose fall the Indians raised a yell and retreated.*

Johnson made political hay off the Battle of the Thames, especially the claim that he killed Tecumseh. In 1814, he went back to the House in triumph as a war hero.

Johnson served until 1819, when he was elected to the state House of Representatives. He served out the term of U.S. Senator John J. Crittenden, who had resigned, and the legislature reelected him to the Senate, where he served from 1819 to 1837, according to the *Kentucky Encyclopedia*.

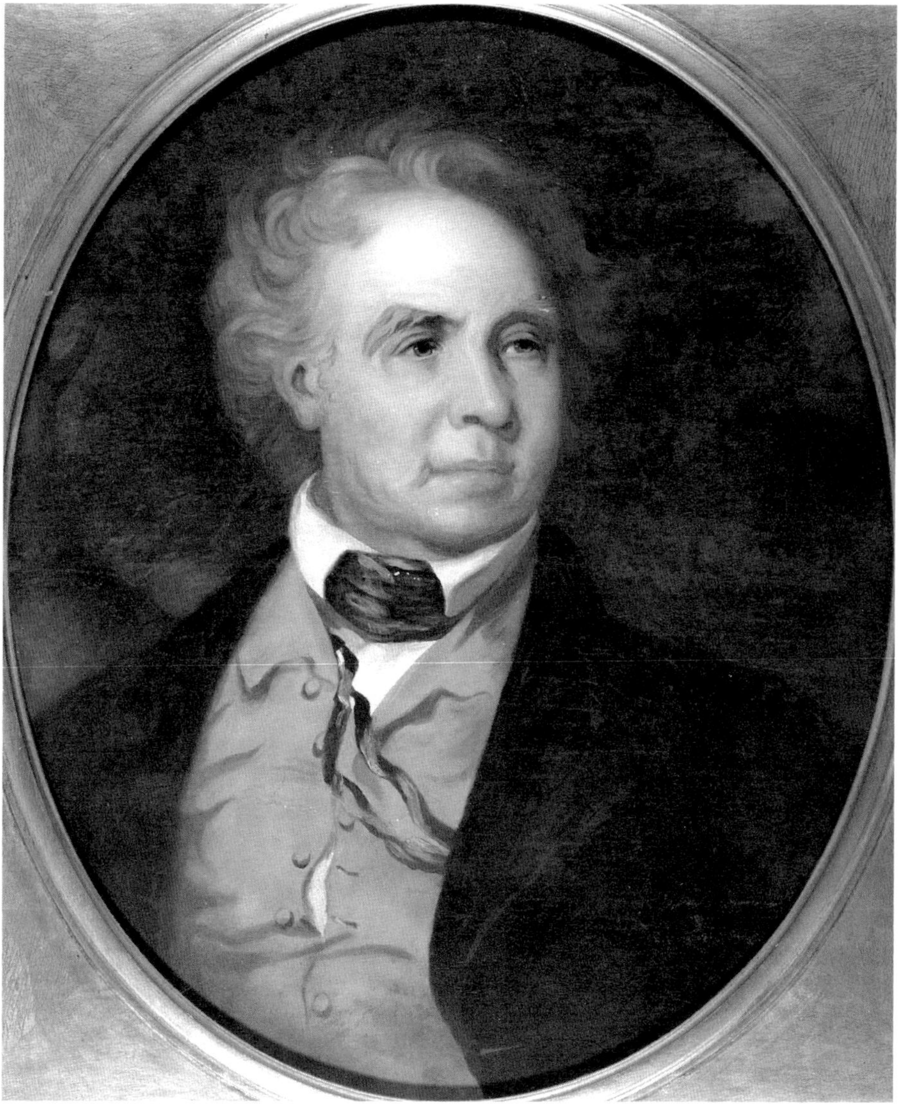

Richard M. Johnson (1781–1850). *Courtesy of the Kentucky Historical Society.*

Johnson was a strong supporter of President Andrew Jackson, who chose Vice President Martin Van Buren to succeed him in 1836. Old Hickory also persuaded the Democratic national convention to nominate his senate ally Johnson for vice president.

Not everybody approved of Kentucky's "Hero of the Thames." Some southern delegates hated Johnson for "openly living with his slave mistress and raising their two daughters pretty much as his own," Klotter said. According to Paul F. Boller Jr.'s book *Presidential Campaigns*, Virginia's delegation stormed out of the hall over Johnson's nomination, hissing "most ungraciously."

Nonetheless, most Democrats supported their party's ticket against a trio of Whigs, including General William Henry Harrison, who led American forces at the Battle of the Thames. But Boller added that the Whigs wondered if "a lucky shot, even if it did hit Tecumseh, qualifies a man for vice president."

Harrison ousted Van Buren for the presidency in 1840 and Johnson came home to Scott County. He served two more terms in the state House of Representatives, died in office in 1850 at age sixty-nine and was buried in the Frankfort Cemetery. "His career as a legislator, was scarcely less brilliant and useful, than that in which he distinguished himself as a warrior," Collins wrote.

In 1843, the General Assembly created Johnson County, naming it for old Rumpsey Dumpsey.

"I NEVER SHOOT ANY RIFLE BUT MY OWN"

The first time he ran for office, Henry Clay found it handier to shoot straight with a rifle than with the voters. Clay, from Lexington, was Kentucky's most famous politician. Dubbed "Gallant Harry of the West," he was a Speaker of the Kentucky House and the U.S. House, secretary of state, senator, three-time presidential candidate and author of a trio of compromises to save the Union.

All of that was ahead of him in 1803, when he tossed his hat into the ring for state representative from Lexington. Clay was twenty-six and apparently unwise in the ways of Kentucky politics. Not until the third and last day of voting—by voice in those days—did he face the electorate.

He had been tarrying at fashionable Olympian Springs in Bath County, according to *Henry Clay: Statesman of the New West*. "It is more likely that he had been cocksure of his election than indifferent to it," author Mayo added.

Clay, a lawyer, made his maiden political speech at Maxwell Spring in Lexington, a popular spot with candidates, according to Clark. The site of the spring, long ago filled in, is on the University of Kentucky campus near the student center, said Clark, who taught history at UK for many years.

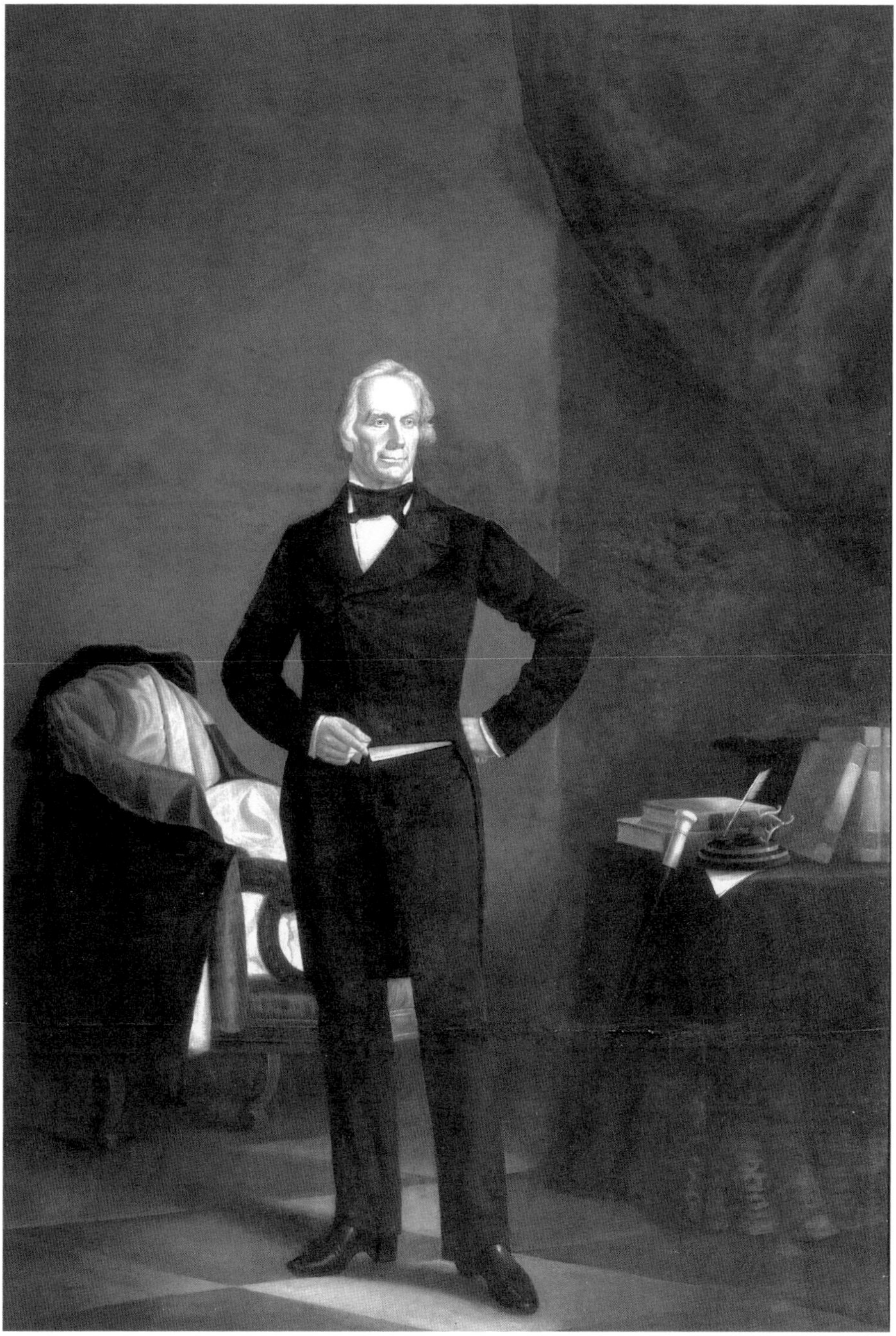

Henry Clay (1777–1852). *Courtesy of the Kentucky Historical Society.*

Facing the voters for the first time, Clay was confronted by a constituent—a buckskin-clad militia man—who wanted to know if he was handy with a rifle. "Being a good shot was the mark of a man," Clark explained. "Clay was a terrible shot."

Even so, Clay bragged that he could outshoot anybody in the country. Prove it, the citizen-soldier demanded. "I never shoot any rifle but my own," Mayo quoted Clay's comeback. The militia man volunteered his weapon, "Old Bess," which he claimed "never fails in the hands of a marksman."

Clay gulped. "Then his gambling instinct asserted itself," Mayo wrote. Clay raised the long flintlock rifle to his shoulder, aimed and fired. He holed the target, eighty yards distant, almost dead center.

The crowd cheered, except for a solitary spoilsport. "Oh, a chance shot!" he sneered, according to Mayo. "Make him try it over."

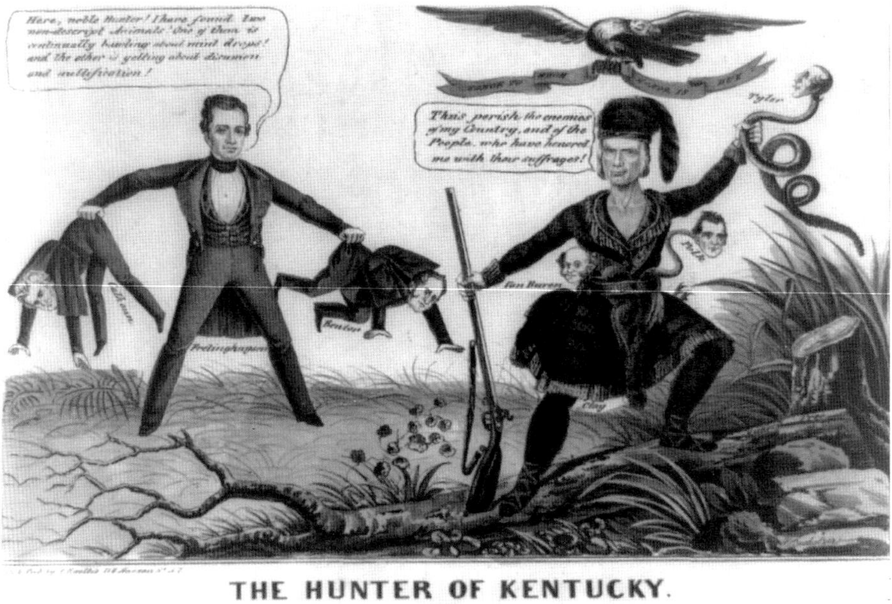

Henry Clay is the hunter and various Democrats his quarry. He grasps a rattlesnake with the head of incumbent president John Tyler. In his belt are two trophies, the Van Buren fox and Polk goose. He stands on the trunk of a felled "Hickory" tree (an allusion to Democratic patriarch Andrew Jackson), while an eagle hovers over him displaying a ribbon with the Whig campaign slogan, "Honor To Whom Honor Is Due." Clay says, "Thus perish the enemies of my Country, and of the People, who have honored me with their suffrages!" To the left stands Clay's running mate, Theodore Frelinghuysen, holding John C. Calhoun and Thomas Hart Benton by the seats of their trousers. J. Baillie, 1844. *Courtesy of the Library of Congress.*

Clay was crestfallen. "Another hit…would have been asking too much of Henry's beloved Goddess of Chance," Mayo wrote. But Clay was, after all, a poker player. He called the heckler's bluff: "Beat that, beat that, and then I will."

The heckler skulked away as the crowd roared for Clay. "Chance shot or not, this young lawyer was a man of spirit, a candidate after their own hearts," Mayo wrote. "So reasoned Old Bess's buckskin owner and his comrades as they marched noisily off to the polls."

Clay won the election, the first of many in which he would triumph. Though he would fight duels with pistols, Clay vowed that he never fired a rifle before or after that fateful day at Maxwell Spring.

"Banners Droop, Bells Toll, Cannons Boom and Funeral Draperies Wave"

The first person to lie in state at the U.S. Capitol was a three-time presidential loser from Kentucky. Henry Clay deserved the tribute, according to Eric Brooks, curator at Ashland, Clay's historic Lexington mansion.

Though Clay failed to win the White House in 1824, 1832 and 1844, his stature as a political leader eclipsed most presidents of his day. "Henry Clay was the model for future lying-in-states, starting with Abraham Lincoln," Brooks said.

Clay was a secretary of state, Speaker of the U.S. House and a U.S. senator. He is most famous for three compromises to save the union and stave off civil war.

Lincoln, a Kentucky native, idolized Clay, praising him as "my beau ideal of a statesman." There are other parallels between the funerals of Clay, the Great Compromiser, and Lincoln, the Great Emancipator.

Clay and Lincoln both died in Washington and were mourned nationwide. After funeral rites in Washington, their remains were taken to their hometowns by special trains, which traveled roundabout routes through major cities.

Lincoln, a Kentucky native, was assassinated in 1865 at age fifty-six. Clay died in 1852; he was seventy-five.

Lincoln was entombed in Springfield, Illinois. Clay was laid to rest in Lexington.

Milward Funeral Directors of Lexington took charge of Clay's interment. Founded in 1825, the family firm is still in business.

"Clay's body was put inside a Fiske Coffin," Brooks said. "It was the cutting edge of coffin technology for its day." The *New York Times* reported

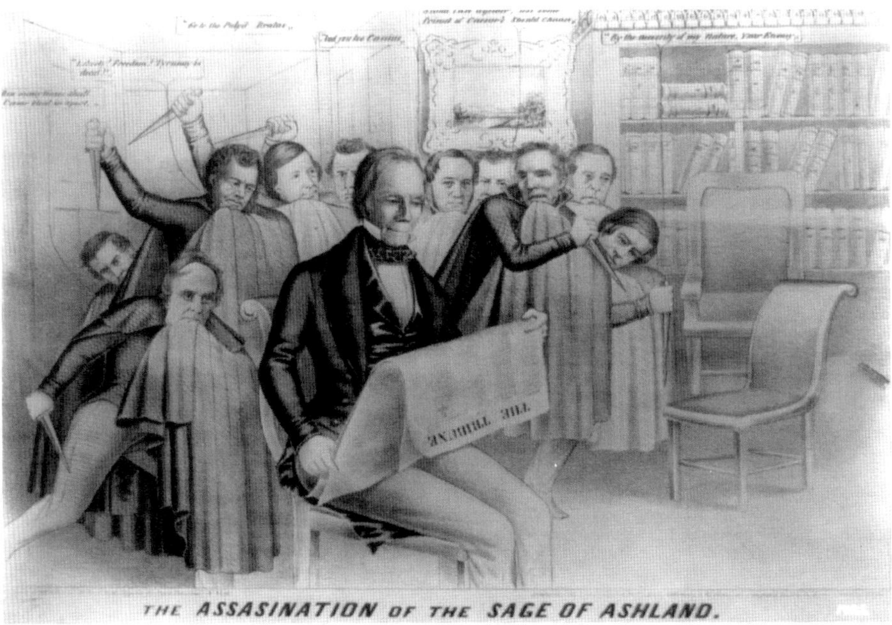

"The assassination of the sage at Ashland." The artist conveys some of the profound disappointment and anger among Henry Clay's many supporters at the nomination of Zachary Taylor at the June 1848 Whig convention in Philadelphia, which was seen as a betrayal of the elder Whig statesman. Clay is pictured seated in the library of his estate at Ashland in Kentucky, reading the *New York Tribune*, whose editor Horace Greeley was a Clay stalwart. Ten men with raised daggers prepare to attack him from behind. These include various Whig powers Daniel Webster, editor James Watson Webb, former New York mayor William V. Brady, Pennsylvania congressman David Wilmot, Kentucky senator and former Clay ally John J. Crittenden and New York state party boss Thurlow Weed. *Courtesy of the Library of Congress.*

that the casket featured "silver handles and mountings, a moveable silver plate over the face, and a massive silver plate bearing the simple inscription of 'Henry Clay.'"

Brooks said that the faceplate covered a small glass window. "The idea was to avoid an accidental burial, which actually happened from time to time," he said. "If the deceased were really only unconscious or comatose, you would be able to see the breath on the glass."

President Millard Fillmore and a host of other politicians and dignitaries jammed the Senate chamber for Clay's memorial service on July 1, 1852. At that moment, Clay was in the thoughts and prayers of citizens nationwide, according to the *Times*.

"In many cities banners droop, bells toll, cannons boom and funeral draperies wave," the newspaper reported.

In crowded streets and on surrounding wharfs, upon steamboats and upon cars, in fields, in workshops, in houses, in schools, millions of men, women and children have their thoughts fixed upon this scene and say mournfully to each other this is the hour in which at the Capital the Nation's representatives are burying Henry Clay.

Clay's Lexington rites were on July 10, 1852, at Christ Church, an Episcopal house of worship where he was a member. Clay is entombed in Lexington Cemetery beneath a 130-foot monument. The marker has been a local landmark since it was finished in 1861, the first year of the Civil War, the bloody conflict between North and South that Clay strove so hard to prevent.

Lincoln, who became president in 1861, eulogized Clay in the 1852 memorial service in Springfield:

Our country is prosperous and powerful; but could it have been quite all it has been, and is, and is to be, without Henry Clay? Such a man the times have demanded, and such, in the providence of God was given us.

"The Devil" Humphrey Marshall

It has been a while since a Frankfort mob threatened to toss a politician in the Kentucky River or ran him out of town with rocks and brickbats. Apparently, the last time was 1795, when U.S. Senator Humphrey Marshall came home, according to Bryant. "Marshall has been described as a vituperative, vitriolic little toad," he said. "He seemed to enjoy making people mad at him."

Bryant doubts that any lawmaker will earn a soaking or stoning in the next session of the General Assembly. "In his day, Humphrey Marshall was probably the most hated man in Kentucky," he said.

Marshall was a Federalist; Kentucky was mainly Jeffersonian. Worse, Marshall voted for the controversial Jay's Treaty, a pact that Thomas Jefferson and his supporters considered treason or close to it. "When Marshall got back to Frankfort, an angry mob was waiting for him," Bryant said.

Born in Virginia in 1760, Marshall was a brother-in-law of John Marshall, first chief justice of the U.S. Supreme Court. After he fought in the Revolutionary War, Humphrey Marshall settled in Frankfort and was elected to the state House of Representatives in 1793.

The next year, the legislature elevated him to the U.S. Senate. Nationally, the Federalists were popular. "Humphrey Marshall was also brilliant, colorful and wealthy," Bryant added. "That would have helped even the devil himself in Kentucky."

To many Kentuckians, Marshall was the devil. The Federalist curmudgeon was a notorious infidel. "His personal letters and papers were so atheistic in tone that his family later burned every scrap they could get their hands on," Bryant said.

Meanwhile, the Frankfort mob burned to get its hands on Marshall. "They manhandled him down to the river and planned to flat dunk him," Bryant said. *A New History of Kentucky* says that Marshall planned to stay dry by appealing to the Baptists in the crowd.

"According to Baptist rules it is irregular to administer baptism before the receiver gives his experience," the senator reminded them. "If you are determined to proceed, let the exercise be performed in decent order. Let me give my experience first." Authors Harrison and Klotter added that "the concept was so ludicrous that the mob dissolved in laughter."

But Marshall was far from home free, according to Bryant. He said that other irate citizens grabbed rocks and brickbats and stoned the senator out of town.

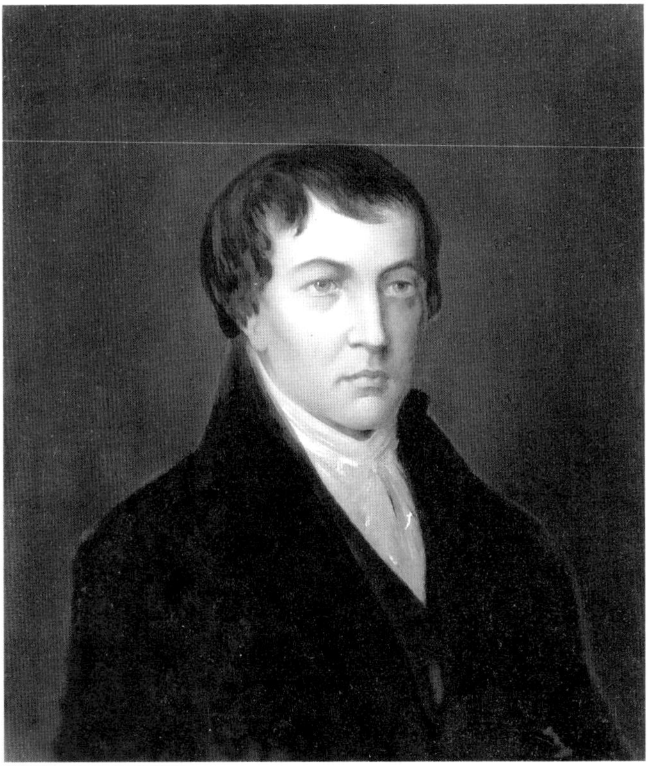

Humphrey Marshall (1760–1841). *Courtesy of the Kentucky Historical Society.*

Marshall survived and was reelected to the state House in 1807 and 1808 but was expelled. Voted back in 1809, Marshall again landed in hot water by goading House Speaker Henry Clay into a duel in which the combatants slightly wounded each other.

Eventually, Marshall forsook politics for publishing. He edited the Frankfort *Western World* and authored *History of Kentucky*, published in 1812 and again in 1824. "He used his paper and his book to vindicate himself and smear his enemies," Bryant said.

Marshall died in 1841 on his Frankfort farm, Glen Willis. His son, Humphrey Marshall Jr., grew up to step to a different drummer, too. While Kentucky remained loyal to Union in the Civil War, Marshall Jr. was a Confederate general.

Rowan County Was Named for a Democratic Duelist

Maybe the bullet that slew Dr. James Chambers in a famous duel near Bardstown in 1801 wasn't the shot heard 'round the world. But it helped inspire a provision in the 1850 Kentucky constitution that required officeholders to solemnly swear that they had never fought a duel. The state's current constitution, ratified in 1891, also has an anti-dueling oath.

John Rowan beat a murder rap for killing Chambers. Afterward, he was a Kentucky secretary of state, congressman, state representative, court of appeals judge and U.S. senator. Rowan County was named for the pistol-packing Jeffersonian Republican turned Jacksonian Democrat whom Lewis and Richard Collins's *History and Kentucky* chronicled as "an able jurist and statesman and one of the most distinguished men in the western country."

Also, Rowan owned "My Old Kentucky Home," which he called Federal Hill. The brick mansion is preserved in a state park in Bardstown, the Nelson County seat. He is buried on the grounds.

My Old Kentucky Home is probably Bardstown's most popular tourist attraction. Seldom visited is the dueling ground where Rowan fatally wounded Chambers just after sunup on February 3, 1801. A green metal state historical society marker on U.S. 31E points out the field of honor about a mile south of Bardstown.

"It's down below the marker on the bank of Beech Fork of the Salt River," said David H. Hall, a Bardstown historian. "It was far enough from town that they could fight a duel and not be disturbed." The Rowan-Chambers duel stemmed from a drunken brawl between the two young men in a Bardstown tavern on January 29, 1801. Important local citizens, Rowan and Chambers had been friends.

A successful lawyer, the Pennsylvania-born Rowan had helped draft Kentucky's second constitution in 1799. He prided himself as a Latin scholar. Well educated, too, Chambers was a popular physician.

The duo had been playing cards and drinking beer. Rowan's luck was better, according to J. Winston Coleman's book *Famous Kentucky Duels*. Coleman quoted Rowan, who claimed that he "won about 11½ dollars on credit from the Doctor besides several quarts of beer."

Tempers rose—Chambers's from losses, Rowan's from too much brew. Insult was heaped on injury when the two started arguing over who knew the most Latin.

Words turned to blows. Rowan, Coleman wrote, was so beery that he landed as many or more punches on a nearby fireplace as he did on the doctor. Apparently, the only injury was Rowan's dislocated thumb from frequent contact with the chimney, Coleman added.

Chambers called Rowan a coward. "Liar," Rowan responded. Two days after their donnybrook, Chambers demanded a duel to settle the score. According to Coleman, if Rowan refused, Chambers vowed "to 'publish' him as a coward in every newspaper in Kentucky" or spread the word about the craven lawyer via handbills.

Rowan accepted the challenge. Their friends tried to head off the showdown but to no avail. It would be pistols at dawn on February 3.

At the appointed hour, the two men, their seconds and some close friends met in a misty clearing next to where a road forded Beech Fork. Grimly, Rowan and Chambers loaded their handmade flintlock dueling pistols. They took their marks ten paces apart, their backs to each other, awaiting the command to fire.

When "fire" was shouted, the men turned but hesitated before pulling the trigger, according to *Famous Kentucky Tragedies and Trials*. The book quotes John Bibb, Rowan's second, who witnessed the duel:

> *Mr. Rowan* [fired] *first, and then the doctor. Mr. Rowan rested his pistol on his left hand—the Doctor on his left arm above the elbow. The deliberate and long aim of each prompted each of their friends to ask if they were hurt.*

Both replied they were uninjured. Neither was hit.

Rowan called for a second round. Chambers agreed.

Again, the doctor failed to hit Rowan. But Rowan's aim had improved; his ball struck Chambers just below the left arm. He slumped to the ground.

Bibb said he told Rowan that Chambers's wound was probably fatal. "I am sorry," Rowan replied, according to Bibb.

The two combatants had ridden horses to the dueling ground. Before he left, Rowan "offered to send his carriage for the doctor," Bibb said.

Meanwhile, Bibb mounted a horse and galloped away to Bardstown to fetch a doctor. He "returned as soon as possible with Dr. Chapieze."

Spirited to his home, Chambers died. Rowan, back at Federal Hill, faced an angry mob bent on avenging what they believed was a coldblooded murder. Fearing for his life, Rowan dressed one of his slaves in his hat and cloak and sent him off on horseback. Rowan sneaked away to some nearby cliffs and hid while the mob chased the slave, Coleman wrote.

Following the duel, rumors swirled. One had it that Rowan got the drop on Chambers, turning first and shooting the doctor in the back. According to another version, Coleman wrote, Rowan had tried to save himself with a bulletproof vest—a quire of heavy paper hidden under his coat.

In any event, Rowan was charged with murder and arrested. State law already forbade dueling, but witnesses said the fight was fair and Rowan was released.

Rowan's son, John Jr., inherited his father's dueling pistol and the old judge's Federal Hill. "John Jr. is supposed to have fought a couple of duels himself," Hall said.

Otherwise hospitable, John Jr. is said to have hosted his composer-cousin Stephen Collins Foster at Federal Hill about 1852. The Rowan Mansion supposedly inspired Foster to write "My Old Kentucky Home," which became Kentucky's state song.

Long after the Rowan-Chambers duel, blueblood hotbloods continued to ignore the law against dueling. "In 1849 the delegates to the constitutional convention inserted a provision in the new charter that required all state officers to take an oath that they had never fought, issued a challenge, or acted as a second in a duel," Robert M. Ireland wrote in the *Kentucky Encyclopedia*. A proscription against dueling, expanded to mean feuding, bushwhacking and street shooting as well, was put in the state's current constitution, which was ratified in 1891.

Kentucky is apparently the only state in which elected officials from the governor down must swear that they have never dueled or abetted duelists.

"One-Arm John"

Did the loss of an arm make John Pope a political power "of great native vigor of intellect"? "One-Arm John" Pope was a nineteenth-century

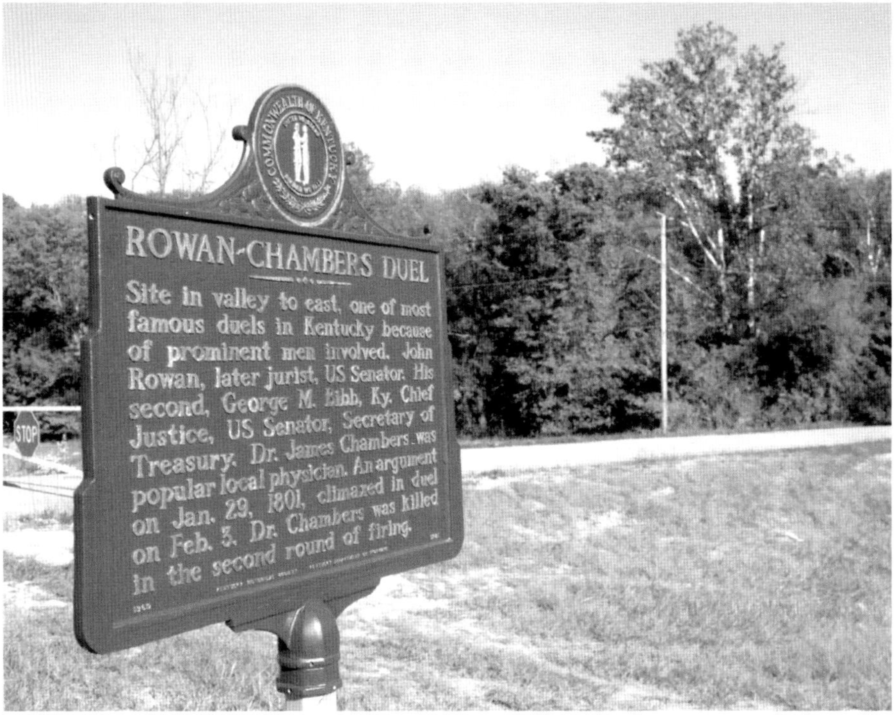

The Rowan-Chambers duel is immortalized with this marker in Nelson County.

Kentucky legislator, secretary of state, congressman and U.S. senator. He was also territorial governor of Arkansas.

"In early life, while attending a cornstalk mill [on his father's farm], he had the misfortune to lose his [right] arm—an accident which turned his attention to the profession of the law," Lewis and Richard Collins wrote in *History of Kentucky*.

Born in Virginia in 1770, Pope lived his last years in Springfield. He is buried in the Washington County seat, where he died in 1845.

Supposedly, Pope's father believed his son could not farm with just one arm, so he encouraged him to become a lawyer. The law apparently whetted Pope's appetite for politics.

Politics and the law required considerable writing. Pope coped.

"He usually had someone else write for him…a document of any length, which he would then sign," said Patrick Snadon, a University of Cincinnati professor, author and authority on Pope Villa, Pope's old home in Lexington. "In the case of shorter memos, his writing and signature was very labored and awkward—like someone who was naturally right-handed but had taught himself with difficulty to write with his left hand."

In 1779, Pope moved with his family to Kentucky, wrote Todd Estes in the *Kentucky Encyclopedia*. He became a prosperous Lexington attorney.

Pope's "political career began in 1800 in Kentucky's electoral college, where he voted for Thomas Jefferson," the encylopedia explains. According to Lewis and Richard Collins, "Being a young man of great native vigor of intellect, he soon attained eminence."

A Democratic Republican, Pope served in the state House of Representatives in the early 1800s. He was a U.S. senator from 1807 to 1813 and Senate president pro tempore in 1810, the encyclopedia notes.

Pope got in political hot water with Kentuckians for opposing the War of 1812. The conflict was popular in the Bluegrass State.

"His explanation that war should have been declared against France as well as Britain and his claim that he would have supported a declaration of war against both belligerents went unheeded in the state," wrote James Wallace Hammack Jr. in *Kentucky and the Second American Revolution: The War of 1812*.

Pope did not run for reelection in 1813. He was Kentucky secretary of state from 1816 to 1819, and in 1825 the voters sent him to the Kentucky Senate, the encyclopedia says.

In 1829, President Andrew Jackson tapped Pope to head the Arkansas Territory. Governor Pope hoped that Arkansas might become "a bright star in the political constellation," according to the online *Encyclopedia of Arkansas History and Culture*.

Pope ended up a Jackson critic, leading Old Hickory to reject him for another term in 1835. Arkansas statehood came the next year. Pope County, Arkansas, is named for the Kentuckian.

When Pope returned to Kentucky, he settled in Springfield and won election to Congress on the Whig ticket. He was in office from 1837 to 1843 but was defeated for reelection and retired, the encyclopedia says.

"Left-Hand Doin's Won't Run Up Hyar"

When Bob Letcher fiddled, the opposition burned. "He might have been the first politician in Kentucky to use music in his campaigns," Klotter suggested.

The music worked like a charm until John C. Breckinridge made Letcher hit a sour note.

An old violin was Letcher's constant companion. Whenever a political opponent spoke in his presence, Letcher would stroll away, Pied Piper like, and saw off a few tunes. The crowd would follow, leaving his foe fuming.

Born Robert Perkins Letcher in Virginia in 1788, he settled in Lancaster, the Garrard County seat. Letcher became a lawyer and a politician. He was a state legislator, congressman and governor between 1814 and 1844. Afterward he was U.S. minister to Mexico. "He was the kind of politician who could keep an audience enthralled for hours with his colorful speeches," Klotter said.

A veteran Whig, Letcher outfoxed Democrats time and again with his famous fiddle. They scorned him as "Greasy Bob" for his stump shenanigans.

But in 1853, the sixty-five-year-old Letcher met his match in Breckinridge, thirty-two, who would win reelection. He was Kentucky's most outstanding pre–Civil War Democrat.

From Lexington, Breckinridge broke into politics in 1849, winning election to the state House of Representatives. Two years later, he won Henry Clay's old congressional seat.

Breckinridge served in Congress from 1851 to 1855 and was elected vice president in 1856. Three years later, the state legislature elected him to the U.S. Senate, though his term was not to begin until 1861.

The Whigs went all out to unseat Breckinridge in 1853. They figured Letcher was just the candidate to beat him.

What turned out to be Letcher's close encounter of the worst kind came in a poor county on the hilly rim of what is now the Sixth Congressional District. Breckinridge and Letcher were to speak together.

Breckinridge knew that Letcher was left-handed. But the congressman put out the word that his challenger fiddled right-handed in wealthy, highfalutin Bluegrass counties.

Sure enough, Letcher sauntered off and struck up a fiddle tune, left-handed, as soon as Breckinridge started to speak. Baited by Breckinridge, Clark wrote in his book *The Rampaging Frontier*, the hill men turned on Greasy Bob.

"Why don't you fiddle with that t'other hand o' yourn?" yelled a "six-footer, in homespun, walnut-dyed clothes, with wild-looking eyes and a 'coonskin cap," Clark wrote. "T'other hand!" the crowd chorused. "Fire up with that t'other hand!"

Maybe for the first time in his long political career, Bob Letcher was at a loss for words. "Gentlemen, I assure you," Letcher spluttered. "No more honey, old hoss," hollered the coonskin-capped constituent. "We ain't b'ars!"

"T'other hand, t'other hand," the chanting continued.

"Coonskin," Clark wrote, shoved his way through the throng "face up to" Bob Letcher. "T'other hand!" the hill man poured it on.

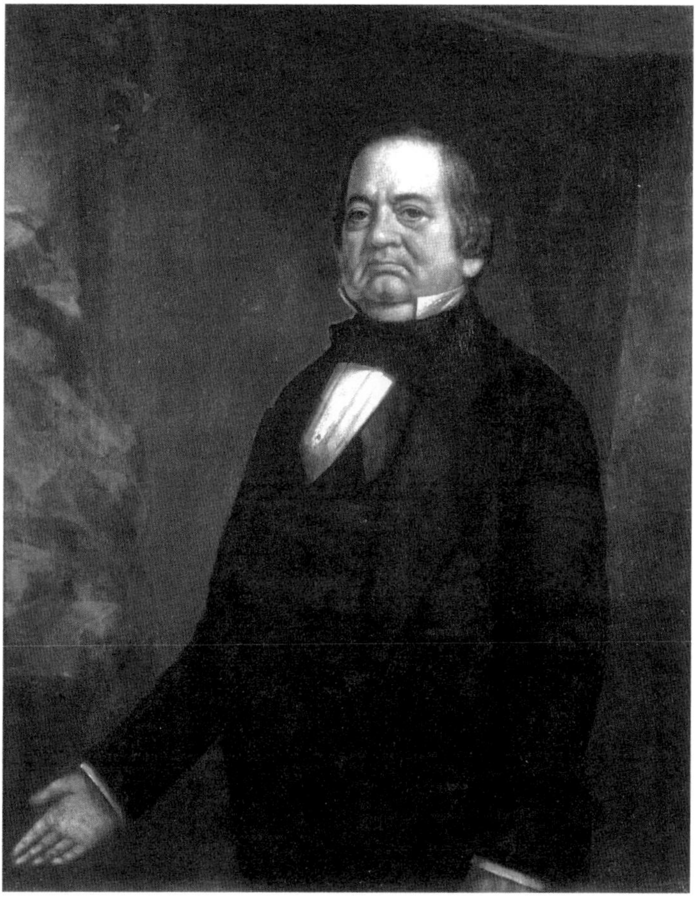

Robert P. Letcher (1788–1861). *Courtesy of the Kentucky Historical Society.*

> *We've heard about you! You fiddle down thar in that d—n Bluegrass country, 'mong rich folks, with your right hand and think when you git up in the hills 'mong poor folks, left handed fiddlin's good enough for them; you've cussedly missed it. Left-hand doin's won't run up hyar; tote out your right, stranger, or look out for squalls!*

Letcher never ran for office again. He died in 1861 and was buried in the Frankfort cemetery.

"Do Not Coil Round Like the Rattlesnake, and Bite Yourself"

Imagine it is one minute past midnight on inauguration day. A congressman from the new president's party inks his pen and starts a twenty-nine-thousand-word good-riddance letter to the outgoing president.

He disses the old president's party as "the most base, cruel, assuming and faithless, that ever disgraced the councils of any nation." He gloats that the party is "now happily humbled in 'dust and ashes, before the indignant frowns of an injured country.'"

Reserving his most poisoned prose for the ex-president, the congressman concludes:

> *I hope and pray that your fate may be a warning to all usurpers and tyrants, and that you may, before you leave this world, become a true and sincere penitent, and be forgiven all your manifold sins in the next.*

Such was the ballistic missive Congressman Matthew Lyon launched against departing President John Adams in 1801. "He was one of the most outspoken members of Congress at a time when political passions were even more powerful than they are today," Klotter said.

The letter has been reprinted several times. J. Fairfax McLaughlin included it in his book *Matthew Lyon: The Hampden of Congress.*

Lyon was a member of Congress from Vermont from 1797 to 1801. Afterward, he moved to western Kentucky, helped found Eddyville and was elected to Congress again in 1803. He served until 1811.

A die-hard Jeffersonian Republican, he detested the Federalist Party of President Adams. It was said that Adams and the Federalists "hated Matthew Lyon as the devil hates holy water."

In Vermont, Lyon also published a ferociously anti-Federalist newspaper called the *Scourge of Aristocracy and the Repository of Important Political Truth.* Lyon's disdain for Adams grew after Lyon was fined and briefly jailed under the Sedition Act of 1798. Passed by a Federalist-majority Congress, the law, in effect, made it a crime to criticize the president.

Reelected while behind bars, Lyon supposedly got even with Adams by making Thomas Jefferson president. In the presidential election of 1800, Jefferson and Aaron Burr tied in the electoral college, so the House of Representatives had to name the winner. On the thirty-sixth ballot, Lyon cast Vermont's decisive vote for Jefferson, Lewis and Richard Collins wrote.

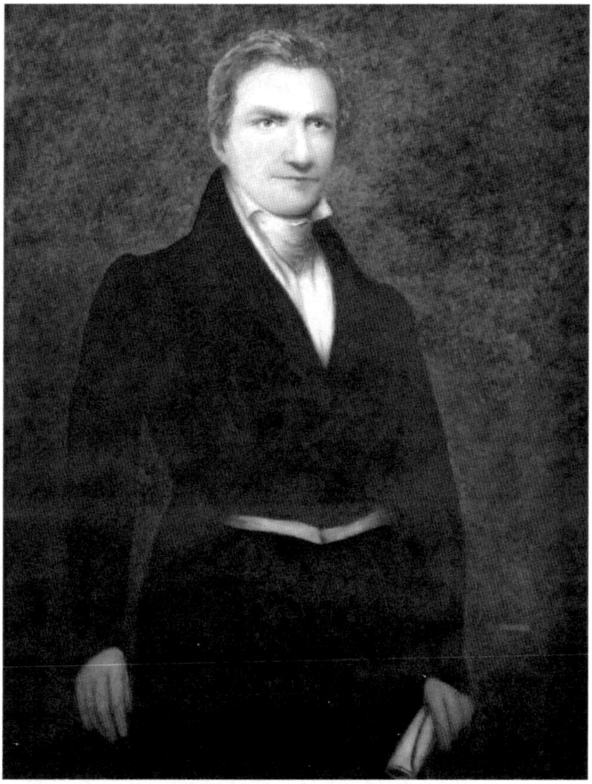

Matthew Lyon (1749–1822). *Courtesy of the Vermont Historical Society.*

Lyon started his version of a Dear John letter at 12:01 a.m. on March 4, 1801, Jefferson's inauguration day. He told Adams he was retiring to Kentucky, a safe haven from the Federalists. He also reminded Adams of the Sedition Act, Adams's "darling hobby horse," according to Lyon.

"You thought by its terrors to shut the mouths of all but sycophants and flatterers, and to secure yourself in the Presidency at least; but how happily have you been disappointed,—the truth has issued from many a patriot pen and press,—and you have fallen, never, never to rise again," Lyon roared.

While the Sedition Act (and companion Alien Acts) would lapse after Jefferson became president, Lyon warned Adams not to cause grief for the new chief executive.

"Your vindictive spirit prompts you to do everything in your power to give the succeeding administration trouble; but you are as unfortunate in this as in most of your calculations," Lyon wrote.

> *Your creatures are generally pliant reeds; they will bend to and fawn upon anybody that is in power. It was power they worshipped in you, not John Adams.*

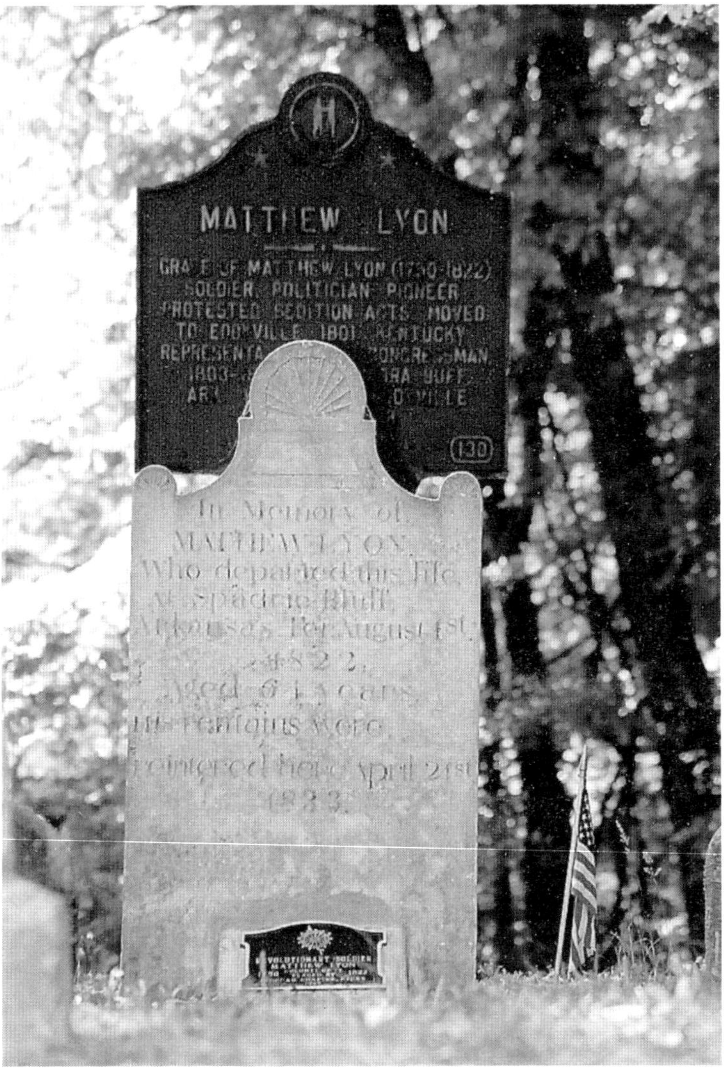

Lyon grave.

Lyon also mockingly urged the ex-president to do himself no harm:

> *Come, pray sir, cool yourself a little. Do not coil round like the rattlesnake, and bite yourself. No, betake yourself to fasting and prayer a while. It may be good for both body and soul. That is a safer remedy for an old man in your situation than the letting of blood.*

"Sound Bite" Had a Different Meaning to "The Spitting Lyon"

Matthew Lyon of Eddyville was a master of the sound bite. The First District's representative in Washington from 1803 to 1811, Lyon said that he got elected by stationing himself "at a cross-roads by which everybody in the district passed from time to time…abusing the sitting member," according to *Henry Clay: Champion of the New West.*

One time, abuse came from a voter named Cofield.

Lyon bit Cofield's thumb off. But it was self-defense.

An Irish-born Vermont congressman before he moved to the Bluegrass State, Lyon belonged to the Jeffersonian Republican Party, a forerunner of the Democratic Party. Eventually, Lyon migrated to western Kentucky, helped found Eddyville (the seat of Lyon County, named for his son, Congressman Matthew Lyon) and got elected to Congress again.

Congressman and constituent came to blows over Cofield's disparaging remarks about the time Lyon spat in the face of a fellow lawmaker, Representative Roger Griswold.

It was on January 30, 1798, when Lyon was a Vermont representative. The Federalists especially hated Lyon. He hated them back.

Lyon focused his fire on Connecticut's Federalists on January 30. He claimed they were a bunch of greedy, power-tripping hypocrites, according to Brian T. Neff's article in *Essays in History*, published online by the University of Virginia's Corcoran Department of History. Lyon also accused the enemy "of brainwashing their constituents with opiates" and bragging "'if he should go into Connecticut, and manage a press there for six months, he could effect a revolution, and turn out the present Representatives,'" Neff added.

Griswold jabbed back. He asked Lyon if he would sport his "wooden sword," a pointed reference to the Jeffersonian's dishonorable, but temporary, discharge from the Continental Army during the Revolutionary War, Neff explained. Lyon was an officer in Ethan Allen's famous Green Mountain Boys regiment.

When Lyon didn't answer Griswold, the Federalist strode over to him. He put his hand on Lyon's arm and repeated the question. "Insulted, embarrassed, and dishonored before his fellow Representatives, Lyon spat straight into Griswold's face," Neff wrote. "Without a word, Griswold wiped the spit with a cloth and exited the chambers."

Griswold apparently figured that Lyon would get kicked out of Congress for his great expectorations. "The Committee of Privileges Instantly drew up a formal resolution calling for the expulsion of Matthew Lyon for 'a violent attack and gross indecency,'" Neff wrote.

But the proposal failed to muster the required two-thirds majority. Griswold, his dander up, determined that his honor had to be avenged.

So about two weeks later, Griswold caught Lyon seated at his desk on the House floor. He whacked Lyon on the head and shoulders with a heavy hickory walking stick, Neff explained.

But Lyon managed to escape to a fireplace, where he grabbed a set of fire tongs. Griswold dropped his cane and grabbed Lyon. The two scuffled until cooler-headed colleagues separated them. One disgusted representative claimed that Congress had thus been degraded to "an assembly of Gladiators," Neff wrote.

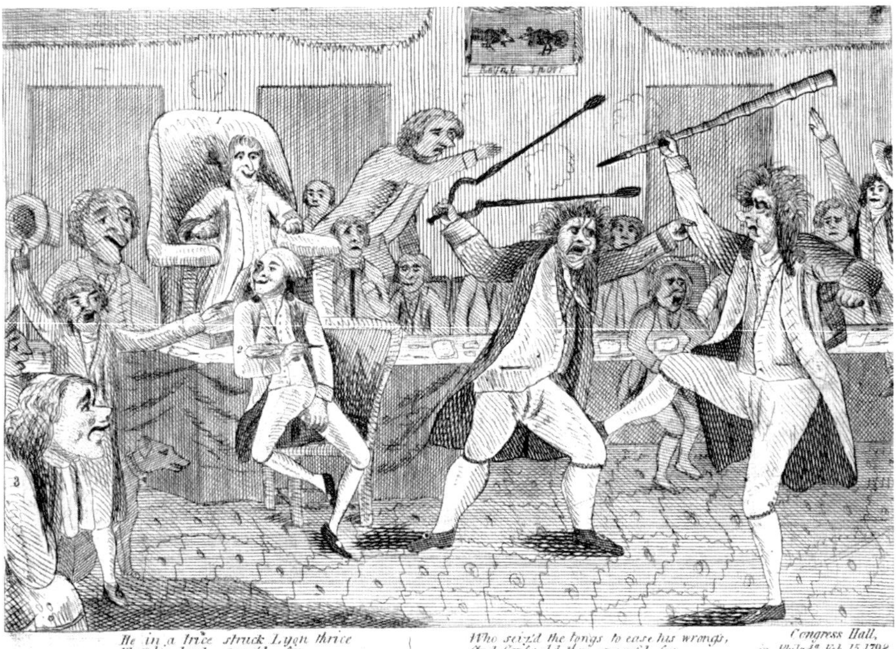

"Congressional Pugilists." A crude portrayal of a fight on the floor of Congress between Vermont representative Matthew Lyon and Roger Griswold of Connecticut. The row was originally prompted by an insulting reference to Lyon on Griswold's part. The interior of Congress Hall is shown, with Speaker Jonathan Dayton and Clerk Jonathan W. Condy (both seated), Chaplain Ashbel Green (in profile on the left) and several others looking on, as Griswold, armed with a cane, kicks Lyon, who grasps the former's arm and raises a pair of fireplace tongs to strike him. Below are the verses: "He in a trice struck Lyon thrice / Upon his head, enrag'd sir, / Who seiz'd the tongs to ease his wrongs, / And Griswold thus engag'd, sir." *Courtesy of the Library of Congress.*

Ever after, Lyon was "the Spitting Lyon."

While Lyon and Griswold basically battled to a draw, Lyon bested Cofield, who, nonetheless, had managed to pin Lyon to the ground. Cofield was all set to deliver the coup de grâce in a backwoods brawl: he aimed his thumb at Lyon's eye, intent on gouging it out.

Somehow, Lyon got the thumb in his teeth "and completely amputated it at the first joint," Mayo wrote in *Henry Clay: Champion of the New West*. The historian added that Lyon, who died at age seventy-three in 1822 and is buried in the old Eddyville cemetery, helped confirm eastern opinions "that Kentucky was truly a paradise for barbarous Yahoos."

"Neither Showed Signs of Relinquishing the Field"

U.S. Representative Chittenden Lyon of Eddyville loved a good political fight, especially if it involved fisticuffs. So the congressman unflinchingly accepted a constituent's challenge to duke it out with him for his vote.

Lyon, the eldest son of the famous Matthew Lyon, "was a man of prodigious physical proportions, being 6-½ feet high in his stockings, and weighing 350 pounds," according to Lewis and Richard Collins's *History of Kentucky*. His foe, Andy Duncan, was "a man of like powerful frame and strength, and nearly as large, and his equal in personal prowess, for both were as game as Old Hickory himself."

Lyon, a Democrat, was a state legislator before he served in Congress from 1827 to 1835. The history book didn't say which campaign featured the dust-up with Duncan, who "bitterly opposed" Lyon. Nonetheless, Duncan pledged his support to Lyon if the candidate "would go out on fair ground, and fight him in a fair old-fashioned Kentucky fist fight," the historians wrote.

Lyon "had braved too many storms, and steered too many flat and keel-boats over dangerous shoals, to be backed down by so fair a proposition!" the authors added. "So, at it they went—Duncan quite confident that he could give the colonel a good trouncing. No easy task, it proved."

The brawl "was long and bloody, and neither showed signs of relinquishing the field or even whispering, 'hold, enough,'" the history book also says.

> *At last, friends parted them, and called it a drawn battle. The contestants washed, took a drink together of Old Robertson whisky (of which they were both fond), shook hands, and made friends for the occasion, as they were personally. Duncan kept his part of the contract, and gave a hearty vote for his jolly competitor in the square stand-up fight.*

Lyon's father was a political warrior, too. When he was a Vermont congressman, Matthew Lyon, a fierce Jeffersonian, spat in the face of a Federalist foe. After he moved to Kentucky and helped found Eddyville, voters sent him back to Congress. When a voter disparaged Lyon over the spitting incident, a scuffle ensued in which Lyon bit off his critic's thumb.

In 1854, the state legislature created Lyon County, naming it for the "Spitting Lyon's" equally combative offspring.

"A Terrible Indictment of a Society that Valued Human Life Too Little and a False Honor Too Much"

Philip Thompson swore that the near-fatal wound he suffered in a duel cured him of rheumatism and a limp. "This particular duel has all the elements of both tragedy and farce," Klotter said.

Robert Triplett shot Thompson, who claimed his assailant "was a good surgeon but severe in remedy."

Early Kentucky was notorious for duels. Yet few gunfights were more bizarre than the Thompson-Triplett tiff of 1829.

The combatants were prosperous attorneys in Owensboro, called Yellow Banks in its pioneer days. Thompson, thirty-nine, was a Mercer County native, War of 1812 veteran and former state legislator and U.S. representative. Triplett, about thirty-three, owned a distillery.

That enterprise brewed the bad blood between Triplett and Thompson, according to *Famous Kentucky Duels*. The two lawyers wrangled; Triplett threatened to cane Thompson, who was physically disabled.

Triplett's brother begged him not "to strike a lame man." Triplett backed off, but he goaded the hot-tempered Thompson into challenging him to a duel, Coleman wrote.

Never mind that as attorneys, Triplett and Thompson were sworn to uphold Kentucky law, which did not allow dueling. They agreed to go pistol-to-pistol in the Indiana backwoods across the Ohio River from Owensboro, the Daviess County seat.

Triplett and Thompson met at the field of honor on February 10, 1829. "Triplett, as the challenged man, named the terms—pistols at ten paces back to back, the parties to whirl and fire between the words *fire* and *three*," Coleman wrote.

Thompson protested; he was too unsteady on his feet to "whirl and fire." He and Triplett assented to stand facing each other.

Each duelist was supplied a pair of hair-trigger flintlock pistols. One of Triplett's two handguns had provided deadly firepower in America's most famous duel. Aaron Burr used the weapon to kill Alexander Hamilton in 1804, Coleman wrote. Triplett and Thompson picked a pistol apiece and squared off at thirty feet. Triplett eyed an aiming point, a greasy smear on the left side of Thompson's greatcoat over the heart.

On command, the combatants fired almost simultaneously. Thompson's shot went wide. Triplett missed his mark but hit Thompson in the right side of his chest.

The wound seemed mortal, "being such as would have killed ninety-nine men out of a hundred," Coleman wrote. Thompson survived, boasting that Triplett's one-ounce lead ball "cured him of chronic rheumatism of ten years' standing, and of his lameness."

Thompson and Triplett became friends. But Thompson, who served in Congress as an Adams-Clay Republican from 1823 to 1825, made other enemies, including a carpenter whom he attacked on an Owensboro street in 1836. The man killed Thompson, apparently in self-defense.

Klotter said that the Triplett-Thompson duel

> *provides a telling example of the extremes to which honor was taken...The picture of a former congressman limping to the dueling ground, and of an opponent who is a man of the law...calmly trying to kill him, is a terrible indictment of a society that valued human life too little and a false honor too much.*

"Like Waving a Red Flag in Front of a Bull"

Willis B. Machen seemed to be asking for trouble.

Yankee gunboats prowled the Cumberland River close to Mineral Mound, his big brick house near Eddyville, the Lyon County seat. Machen raised a Rebel flag anyway.

"That was like waving a red flag in front of a bull," said Odell Walker, a local historian and author. "The Federals couldn't resist taking a potshot."

A 1947 fire, not the Yankees, destroyed Machen's old home. Stone steps and part of the foundation survive near the twelfth green at the Mineral Mound State Park golf course.

Machen was true to his flag. Though Kentucky was officially Union, he and other Southern sympathizers organized a rump Rebel government for the Bluegrass State behind Confederate lines at Russellville in 1861.

Machen "represented" the First District in the Confederate Congress at Richmond, Virginia. He "was a strong legislator and was unwilling to truckle to malcontents and state supreme courts," the *Biographical Register of the Confederate Congress* notes.

Born in 1810, Machen, a lawyer and a Democrat, served in the Kentucky legislature before the Civil War. He helped draft the state constitution of 1850.

After he returned from Russellville, Machen "hoisted the Confederate flag over Mineral Mound," wrote Paducah journalist and historian Hall Allen in his book *Center of Conflict*. "As [Union]…gunboats made their way along the Cumberland to and from Fort Donelson [Tennessee], the Stars and Bars taunted them from the hilltop."

A gunboat fired a cannonball into Machen's living room, Allen added. Evidently, no blood was spilled. "Then, having expressed its sentiments, the gunboat moved on, leaving the Confederate banner still waving in the Lyon County breeze."

When the Civil War ended, Machen fled to Canada, where his family joined him. But according to Allen, President Andrew Johnson pardoned the western Kentuckian and the Machens came home to Mineral Mound.

After the Civil War, Machen served briefly in the U.S. Senate and was a state railroad commissioner. He also farmed and ran iron furnaces, notes the *Kentucky Encyclopedia*.

A state historical marker on Kentucky 93, near the site of Mineral Mound, says that Machen was "a courageous leader of strong convictions and unimpeachable integrity."

Machen died in 1893. Nine years before, his daughter, Minnie, got married at Mineral Mound. "Her daughter was Zelda Sayre Fitzgerald, wife of the famous writer, F. Scott Fitzgerald," said Walker, who lives near Kuttawa, also in Lyon County.

Allen said the cannon shot left Mineral Mound permanently scarred. "On the front wall was a patchwork of brick that did not match the rest of the house," he wrote. "That was where Willis B. Machen plugged up the hole made by a Yankee cannonball."

"HE NEVER DID BELIEVE IN SLAVERY"

A member of Congress who voted to end slavery is buried unheralded in Mayfield, a western Kentucky town his father founded.

Except for a gray marble tombstone in a tiny family cemetery, there are no Mayfield monuments commemorating Representative Lucian Anderson.

Maybe that's because he was a Republican and an abolitionist in one of Kentucky's most Democratic and pro-Confederate communities.

Anderson voted for the Thirteenth Amendment, which forbade slavery. It became part of the constitution in 1865. Anderson was born in Mayfield, the Graves County seat, in 1824. He was the son of John Anderson, who is credited with starting Mayfield in 1823.

Apparently, Lucian Anderson always stepped to a different drummer. He joined the Whig Party.

An attorney, Anderson was a Whig presidential elector in 1852, though Graves County and the nation went for Democrat Franklin Pierce. Even so, voters thought enough of Anderson to elect him county attorney.

After the Whig Party collapsed, Anderson won a term in the state House of Representatives. He served from 1855 to 1857.

When the Civil War broke out in 1861, Anderson was among the few local supporters of the Union. "He never did believe in slavery," said his granddaughter, Margaret Stevens.

Anderson's antislavery and anti-Confederate views jeopardized his life and property. Once, a group of Southern sympathizers threatened to burn his house, an 1854-vintage wooden home that survives as Mayfield's oldest dwelling.

Anderson's wife, Ann Lockridge Anderson, overheard the plotters. "She told them that it was her house, too, and that they had children," Stevens said. "She also said she knew who they were and that if the house was burned, she'd know whom to blame."

Unionists from the First Congressional District sent Anderson to Congress in 1863. Military authorities suspected the majority Democrats of disloyalty. They struck the name Lawrence Trimble of Paducah, Anderson's antiwar Democratic opponent, from the ballot in most counties. Trimble was jailed until after the election.

Anderson became a Rebel captive shortly after the election. In November 1863, "a party of 'Confederates'" grabbed the representative-elect "and retained him in custody until just before the meeting of Congress, then exchanged [him]," according to *Biographical Annals of the Civil Government of the United States from Original and Official Sources* by Charles Lanman.

Besides voting for the Thirteenth Amendment, Anderson was a delegate to the 1864 Republican national convention that renominated Abraham Lincoln. He was one of the founders of the GOP in the Bluegrass State.

After the war, Anderson resumed his Mayfield law practice but not his Washington career. With ex-Confederates and pro-Southern Democrats back in control in western Kentucky, it was evident that Anderson couldn't win another House term.

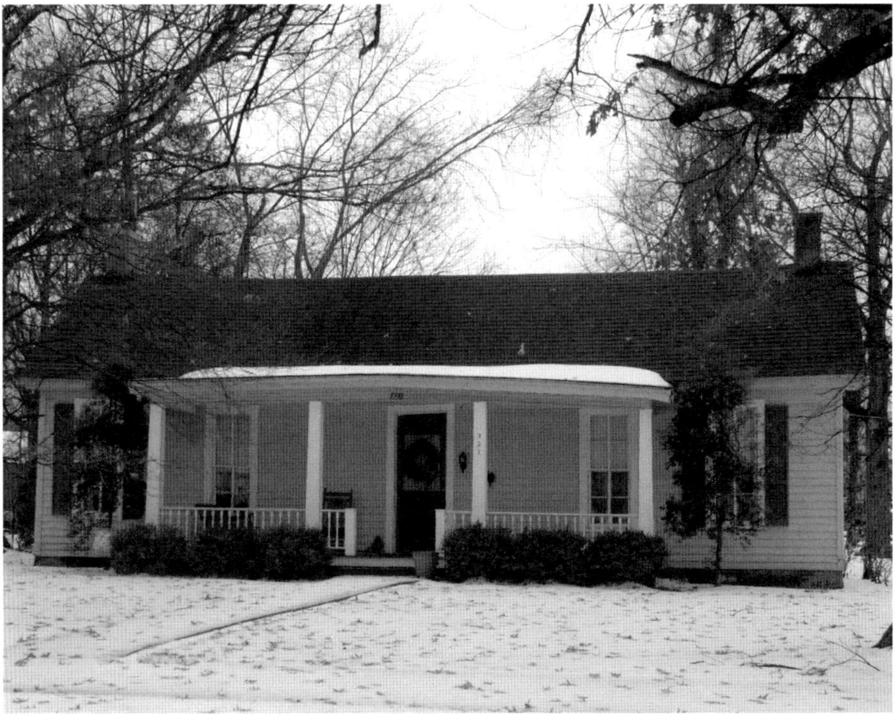

Home of Lucian Anderson, Mayfield, Kentucky.

He didn't try. Trimble beat another Republican and got Anderson's seat. The next year, Lanman wrote, the ex-representative traveled to Philadelphia for the "Loyalists' Convention."

Anderson remained a prosperous Mayfield attorney before he died in 1898.

Like many Kentucky families, the Andersons were split by the Civil War. Lucian's brother, Ervin Anderson, was ardently pro-Southern. It was said that Ann Lockridge Anderson sympathized with the Confederates, too.

"It was a typical Kentucky family," Stevens said. "Some were on one side and some were on the other."

A KENTUCKY REBEL LOST HIS LEG BUT WON A "SWEET GIRL"

A young Confederate officer is wounded in the leg and left on a sunbaked battlefield. A local belle shades the suffering soldier with her shawl. "Her nobleness of character so manifested itself through her gentle manner and kindly words and actions that my heart was completely captured," remembered Captain William J. Stone, who survived the Civil War and served ten years in Congress.

Stone, from Lyon County in western Kentucky, lost his left leg in the Battle of Cynthiana in 1864. But he won a bride.

He ended up marrying his battlefield Samaritan, Cornelia Woodward.

"The story, if told in the shape of a novel, would be considered improbable," the *New York Times* reported. "But truth is stranger than fiction, and there are more romances all around us than there are on the book shelves."

Or on movie screens, said Odell Walker. He prizes a rare copy of the brief, unpublished autobiography Stone wrote after he had left Congress and was Kentucky's commissioner of Confederate pensions. Stone died in 1923 at age eighty-one.

Stone was twenty-two when he was wounded. A veteran of many bloody battles, he was a captain under General John Hunt Morgan, the famous Kentucky cavalry raider from Lexington.

Morgan assaulted Cynthiana, the Harrison County seat, on June 11, 1864. The next day, Union troops counterattacked and forced Morgan to retreat. Stone was among the wounded.

Stone said that he "lay on the battlefield all day" after a Union rifle bullet shattered his right leg. Before his bride-to-be arrived, a Union soldier brought him water.

Stone was "gasping for water, with his leg shot way almost to the hip," the *Times* reported. The erstwhile enemy

> *raised the wounded man, and gave him a drink, and then in kindness left his own canteen by the side of what he thought to be the dying rebel. Said he: "I will leave this, as you may want to drink again after a while."*

Stone added that the soldier also saved him from another Yankee who wanted to kill him. The man threatened to shoot Stone, according to the old Rebel's memoirs. Stone recalled that the Union soldier who had befriended him warned the would-be assailant, "If you do you will be the next one to die; I will kill you as quick as my gun will fire!"

Woodward was one of several young women who tended the wounded, according to the *Times* story, which was published on May 16, 1886.

> *They had gathered the ramrods scattered among the dead, and…* [Woodward] *finding Mr. Stone still alive and the hot sun beating down upon him, took a bundle of these ramrods and stuck them into the earth,*

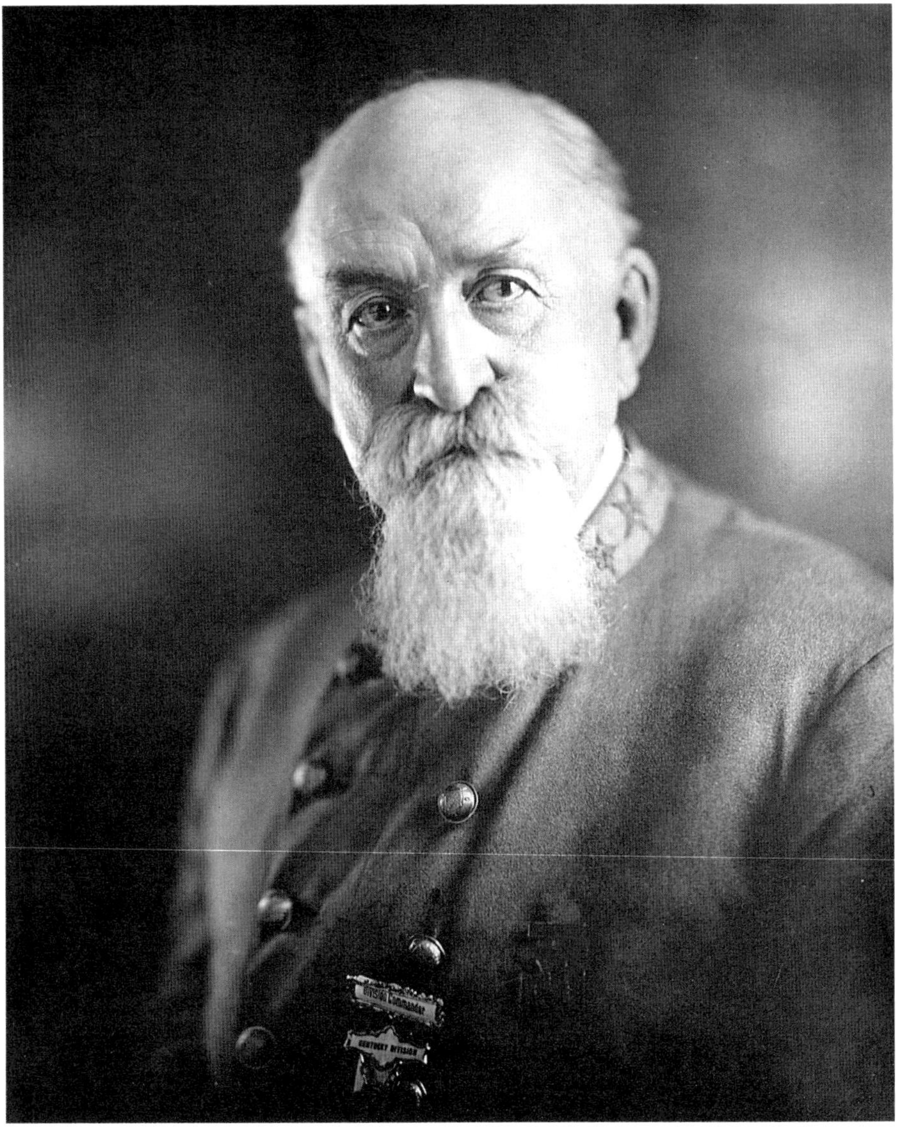

William Johnson Stone. *Courtesy of the Kentucky Historical Society.*

> *making a half moon of paling-fence about his head. Over this she spread her shawl, and did what she could to ease him.*

Stone was taken to a local church that had been converted to a hospital. There were so many injured soldiers that Stone said he "lay without having any attentions to my wound till the morning of the 15th of June."

One of Morgan's surgeons stayed behind to aid the wounded. He amputated Stone's leg on August 11.

Visits from Cornelia lifted the captain's spirits. "This…beautiful young lady often came to administer to the needs of the wounded in whatever way she could," Stone wrote. "She was often at my bedside."

Woodward kept seeing Stone after he was transferred to a house in Cynthiana. After a while, he went home to western Kentucky and became a farmer near Eddyville.

The loss of a limb did not stop him from returning to Cynthiana once the war was over. Fitted with a wooden peg leg, he went to Cornelia, confessed his undying love for her and proposed. On October 29, 1867, Stone wrote, "this sweet girl…became my wife."

The Stones reared two daughters and were married for thirty-nine years. His sweet Cornelia died in 1906. "God called my wife home," Stone remembered. "She went to Heaven to be with the redeemed of the Lord throughout all eternity."

Meanwhile, Stone, a Democrat, had become one of Kentucky's leading politicians. Elected to the state House of Representatives in 1867, 1875 and 1883, he was chosen Speaker in 1875, according to the *Biographical Directory of the United States Congress, 1774–Present.*

In 1884, First District voters sent him to Congress. He served five terms as a populist-minded champion of his region's many small farmers.

In 1899, Stone sought the Democratic nomination for governor. He lost to the controversial William Goebel of Covington, who, in 1900, became the only American governor to be assassinated in office. Stone maintained that Goebel's followers stole the nomination from him "by the most dishonest means ever practiced in a Convention."

Stone married Elizabeth H. Chambers, a widow, in 1909. He said that she was as "kind and thoughtful of my comfort and welfare as it is possible for any wife to be."

But Stone's autobiography reveals that he still adored Cornelia. "No man had a sweeter, nobler, more loving or helpful wife than I," Stone wrote.

> *No children had a more loving, kind and devoted mother…My only regret was that I was not a better husband. It was hard to give her up but my only consolation was that she had gone to Heaven where she would have no more pain and no more sorrow.*

"KILLING A MAN DID NOT NECESSARILY DISQUALIFY ONE FOR OFFICE"

Caleb Powers spent eight years in jail for helping kill a governor. Then he spent eight more in Congress.

"Killing a man did not necessarily disqualify one for office in late nineteenth and early twentieth century Kentucky," Bryant said. "Sometimes, it enhanced one's reputation."

Powers, a Barbourville Republican, was Kentucky's secretary of state in 1900, when he reputedly masterminded the shooting of Governor William Goebel, a Covington Democrat. "Powers knew if he could escape the hangman, he would be assured of his party's support," Bryant said.

Indeed, voters in Powers's traditionally Republican eastern Kentucky district elected the ex-con to Congress four times. He was in office from 1911 to 1919.

Nobody knows who killed Goebel. The identity of his murderer—or murderers—is one of the great mysteries of Bluegrass State history.

"What is believed depends on which evidence is accepted," Klotter wrote in the *Kentucky Encyclopedia*. However, Goebel was "the only governor in American history to die in office of wounds inflicted by an assassin," he added.

The Republicans claimed that the Democrats stole the close and controversial 1899 governor's election. The GOP insisted that its man, William S. Taylor of Morgantown, was the real winner. The dispute nearly sparked civil war in Frankfort between gun-toting Republicans and Democrats.

Powers was elected secretary of state in 1899. Supposedly, he headed a GOP cabal to slay Goebel, who was fatally wounded on January 30, 1900, outside the old state capitol. A bronze plaque in the sidewalk marks the spot.

Goebel died on February 3, 1900. Allegedly, he was shot from the window of Powers's office. Powers was out of town, conveniently or otherwise.

"Eventually, of the sixteen people indicted [including Taylor], three turned state's evidence; of the remaining thirteen, only five went to trial," Klotter wrote in the encyclopedia. Two were acquitted. Powers and another pair, including Jim Howard, Goebel's suspected killer, were found guilty but ultimately pardoned.

"All of the convicted men continued to their deaths to proclaim their innocence," Klotter wrote.

Powers defended himself in his autobiography, *My Own Story*. The book was published in 1905.

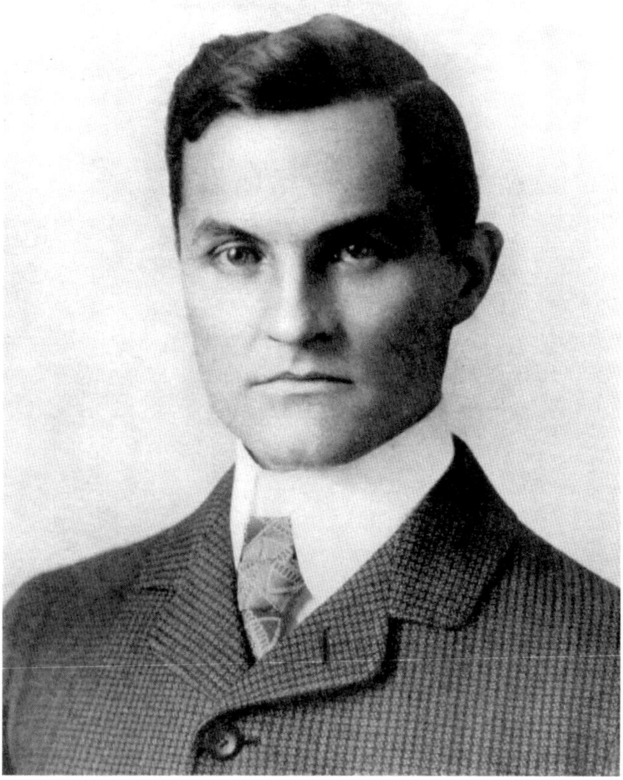

Caleb Powers (1869–1932). *Courtesy of the Kentucky Historical Society.*

Six years later, Powers ran for Congress the first time and won. He didn't seek a fifth term, though Bryant suspects that Powers could have been reelected.

Powers died in 1932 at age sixty-three.

"We know that Powers wanted Goebel out of office," Bryant said. "Did he want him out badly enough to kill him? That remains the question."

"Bright as a Sunbeam and Saucy as a Bowl of Jelly"

Supposedly, former Representative William Preston Taulbee's blood still stains the shiny marble steps in the U.S. Capitol where *Louisville Times* reporter Charles E. Kincaid gunned him down.

"It was big news nationwide," Bryant said.

The February 28, 1890 shooting stemmed from a long-smoldering feud between the two men over a salacious story Kincaid wrote accusing

Taulbee of adultery. Allegedly, the Salyersville Democrat was caught "in a compromising way" with his mistress, "a little daisy," Kincaid claimed. She was "bright as a sunbeam and saucy as a bowl of jelly; petite of figure but plump as a partridge."

Taulbee died on March 11, 1890. He lived long enough, the *Washington Star* reported, to express "no resentment" toward his assailant. But the ex-lawmaker "thought the manner of the shooting was cowardly."

Kincaid confessed to killing the unarmed Taulbee. Charged with first-degree murder, the reporter was hauled into court where two witnesses swore they saw him shoot the ex-congressman. In yet another strange twist to the tale, the jury found Kincaid not guilty, ruling it a case of self-defense.

Meanwhile, Taulbee had kept quiet about the alleged tryst. "Taulbee blamed Kincaid for ruining his career and his personal life, but he evidently did not confirm or deny the charge of infidelity in Kincaid's story," Bryant said.

The historian added that Kincaid even promised Taulbee, a former Methodist minister, ample space in the *Times* to refute his account of the affair. "Apparently, Taulbee never took Kincaid up on his offer," Bryant said.

Dubbed "the Mountain Orator," Taulbee was elected to the U.S. House in 1884. After Kincaid's story ran in the *Times* in 1888, Taulbee decided against a third term. He became a Washington lobbyist. He and his wife of seventeen years also separated, according to Klotter, Kentucky state historian.

Taulbee became the sworn enemy of Kincaid, who had been private secretary to Governor Proctor Knott, a Democrat. After a scuffle with Taulbee, the reporter said that he decided to steer clear of the ex-congressman, Klotter wrote in a 1980 issue of the *Historian*, a scholarly journal.

Taulbee, thirty-nine, and Kincaid, five years his foe's junior, clashed twice at the Capitol before the reporter shot the lobbyist. The first encounter was bloodless, beginning with heated words and ending with Taulbee yanking Kincaid's ear, Klotter wrote. A pair of doorkeepers pried the combatants apart.

Before going their separate ways, Kincaid told Taulbee that he was "a small man and unarmed." The strapping Taulbee, about a foot taller than the frail, five-foot, three-inch Kincaid, warned the reporter that "he had better arm himself," Klotter wrote.

Kincaid took Taulbee's advice. When the men met again two hours later on the steps leading to a basement restaurant, Kincaid produced a revolver and shot Taulbee in the head, close to his eye.

Bleeding profusely, Taulbee staggered a few steps and collapsed into the arms of a Capitol police officer. Kincaid admitted that he was the shooter and surrendered peacefully.

Louisville newspapers rallied to Kincaid, arguing that Taulbee was a big bully who had repeatedly threatened and abused the little reporter and had even attacked him. "The *Courier-Journal* fueled its Commonwealth's growing reputation for lawlessness by suggesting that 'that which may be regarded in Kentucky and other states of the Union as a matter of self-defense is treated here in Washington as murder in the first-degree,'" Klotter wrote. "As it developed, the District of Columbia's code apparently did not differ from Kentucky's after all: Kincaid was acquitted."

"By Wiles and Artifices and Protestations of Affection"

"She was a woman of passion," Representative William Campbell Preston Breckinridge said of Madeline V. Pollard. "I was a man of passion. We yielded ourselves to each other. That was all."

There was more. In 1893, Pollard sued Breckinridge, her lover, for breach of promise in Washington and won. The scandal finished him politically.

The Lexington Democrat had been a rising star in Congress. After he was elected to a fifth term in 1892, Breckinridge was talked up "as the next Speaker of the House if that body became Democratic, or as a cabinet-level appointee, or as a candidate for the vice presidency," Klotter wrote in his book, *The Breckinridges of Kentucky*.

Breckinridge was on his second wife when he and Pollard became paramours. He owned up to the affair but said he never pledged to marry her. Breckinridge was dubbed "the Silver-Tongued Orator." But a Washington, D.C. jury believed Pollard and awarded her $15,000.

Breckinridge was from a famous political family. "The name of Breckinridge, like those of Caesar, Cromwell, Napoleon, is imperishable," wrote John J. McAtee in *Kentucky Politicians: Sketches of Representative Corncrackers and Other Miscellany*. "It shines like a star on the roll of American fame."

Born in Baltimore in 1837, "Billy Breck" was a prosperous Lexington lawyer when the Civil War began. His father, the Reverend Robert J. Breckinridge, and two of his brothers sided with the Union. W.C.P. and Robert Breckinridge Jr. became Confederate officers.

After the war, he was an attorney and newspaper editor in Lexington. Voters elected him to Congress in 1884.

By the time he wed Louise Wing in 1893, Breckinridge had outlived two wives. Pollard claimed that she met Breckinridge by chance on a train in April 1884.

She "was seventeen years old and a student at Wesleyan Female Seminary, in Cincinnati," the *New York Times* reported. Breckinridge, forty-six, was married to Issa Desha Breckinridge, his wife of twenty-three years.

Pollard said that Breckinridge visited her at the seminary in August 1884, "and by wiles and artifices and protestations of affection subsequently took advantage of her youth." The *Times* also said that "the birth of a third child [is] allegedly…the result."

Meanwhile, Breckinridge seemed devoted to Issa and their children. He was a regular churchgoer who rarely smoked, drank liquor, played cards or bet on horses. His secret weakness, Klotter wrote, was Madeline Pollard.

When she got her day in court, Pollard showed up dressed in black and escorted by a nun, according to Klotter. She testified that after Issa died in 1892, the widower Breckinridge promised to wed her. Instead, the *Times* reported, he "wrongfully and injuriously" jilted her for the widow Wing.

The trial grabbed headlines in other newspapers from coast to coast. "There were even books written about it," said Klotter, state historian of Kentucky, author and Georgetown College professor.

Pollard sued for $50,000. The District of Columbia Supreme Court jury awarded her $15,000.

Pollard might have needed the money. She was fired from her government job, allegedly "for making a derogatory remark" about General William T. Sherman when he died, according to the *Times*.

Having lost in court, Breckinridge had to battle for his political life. Accustomed to easy victories at the polls, he faced an army of enemies.

Breckinridge's own Presbyterian Church expelled him for four months. The National Christian League for the Promotion of Social Purity prayed that Congress would expel him. The group also begged Louise to leave him "if she has a spark of womanhood," Klotter wrote. She stuck by him.

Having survived bloody Civil War combat, Breckinridge refused to give up his seat in Congress without a fight. In 1894, he took on two Democratic primary challengers. Breckinridge suspected that one of them, Will Owens, had bankrolled Pollard's suit.

If either opponent was a better man, so be it, Breckinridge tearfully told Democrats in Lexington. Choose "someone whose life has been stainless, whose nights have been sinless," he proposed. "For a hundred years this district has been represented by men. They have not always been sinless men."

Breckinridge finished second to Owens, losing by a mere 255 votes out of 19,299 ballots cast, Klotter noted. "The loss by less than 1 percent of the vote revealed that despite his human errors people still loved their 'Billy Breck.'"

Breckinridge swapped his House seat for an editor's chair at the *Lexington Morning Herald*, which he and his son, Desha Breckinridge, bought. He also practiced law until his death in 1904 at age sixty-seven.

"Kentucky Women Are Not Idiots"

Madeline McDowell Breckinridge was born in Kentucky when women couldn't vote, sue for divorce or own property while their husbands were still alive.

Breckinridge, Henry Clay's great-granddaughter, grew up to fight for equal rights for women. She helped put Kentucky in the column of states that approved the Nineteenth Amendment to the constitution. Ratified in 1920, it guaranteed women the right to vote.

Breckinridge didn't pull punches, even with powerful politicians. "Kentucky women are not idiots—even though they are closely related to Kentucky men," *A New History of Kentucky* quotes her.

"'Madge' Breckinridge was one of the leading suffragists and Progressive reformers in the South," said Melba Hay, author of *Madeline McDowell Breckinridge and the Battle for a New South.* According to *A New History of Kentucky*, Breckinridge was "the most influential woman in the state" in her time.

All the while, Madge Breckinridge skillfully hid a disability. She lost a foot, and possibly part of a leg, to tuberculosis of the bone. Her secret was so well kept that there are no known records of which foot, or leg, was the prosthesis, said Hay.

"She traveled all over the country making speeches on behalf of women's rights," Hay said. "She walked on crutches and sometimes had to be held up when she spoke. In private, she said she was in great pain, but she kept going."

Indeed, tuberculosis plagued Breckinridge for most of her life. At age thirty-two, she also suffered a stroke. She persevered and became president of the Kentucky Equal Rights Association in 1912. In 1913, she was elected vice president of the National American Woman Suffrage Association.

Breckinridge marched, wrote and spoke powerfully for women's rights. She also battled poverty. Breckinridge helped start schools for poor children in Lexington, her hometown. She assisted in the founding of a mission near

Beattyville in the Kentucky mountains, one of the poorest regions in the country, according to the encylopedia.

She led the campaign for a state-run tuberculosis sanitarium in Lexington. She also persuaded the Kentucky General Assembly to adopt a progressive juvenile justice system similar to one she had observed in Denver while recuperating there in a tuberculosis sanitarium.

Breckinridge seldom, if ever, referred to her disability or illness in public, said Hay, who wrote her PhD dissertation on the Bluegrass State suffragist. "She never made reference to it in any speech I know of and there is nothing about it in what I would call her business papers."

Breckinridge never lacked money. But Hay believes that Breckinridge's disability and poor health helped fire her passion for reform. "You can see it in her letters and other writings," Hay said.

Born near Frankfort in 1872, Madeline McDowell was from an old and wealthy Kentucky family. Her great-grandfather was Henry Clay, one of America's greatest nineteenth-century political leaders.

When she was a girl, Madeline lived with her parents at Ashland, Clay's Lexington mansion. Her health troubles began in her teens, when she started suffering unexplained ankle pain.

The ailment mystified doctors in Lexington, Louisville, Cincinnati and New York. They prescribed rubber stockings, cod liver oil, shoes with iron-reinforced soles and heavy, orthopedic boots. "This went on for about five years," Hay said, adding that the pain persisted.

In 1896, Breckinridge returned to New York where doctors at the Hospital for Ruptured and Crippled, now the acclaimed Hospital for Special Surgery, diagnosed her with tuberculosis of the bone. Dr. Virgil P. Gibney, the hospital surgeon in chief, amputated her foot.

"There may have been subsequent surgeries," Hay said. "There is a record that she bought a 'willowood limb' and paid $75 for it."

The amputation did not rid her of tuberculosis. Breckinridge spent long periods in and out of sanitariums. "Back then, the main treatment was fresh air and a high fat, high calorie diet, which may have contributed to her death of a stroke at age 48," Hay said. "At one time, doctors told her to drink a pint of cream a day."

In 1898, Madeline, twenty-five, wed Desha Breckinridge, editor of the influential *Lexington Herald* newspaper. But Madge Breckinridge was not content to live the life of a socialite.

She found a guiding spirit in her sister-in-law, Sophonisba Breckinridge. A Kentucky-born reformer, lawyer, author, professor and pioneering sociologist, she moved to Chicago and became involved in the settlement house movement to help poor immigrants. Sophonisba Breckinridge, also a member of the National Association for the Advancement of Colored People and the Women's Trade Union League, was an ally of Jane Addams, who started the famous Hull House in Chicago.

"Madge would work through Sophonisba to get speakers from Hull House to come to Lexington," said Hay. But Madge Breckinridge is best known as a women's rights champion, the historian added.

"The most influential woman in the state, she used new tactics such as suffrage marches, as well as her speaking ability and humor, to gain more support," Harrison and Klotter wrote.

> *In a strong voice coming from a slim and often weak body, she told audiences to look at male-led Kentucky, with its poor schools, violence, and corrupt politics, and asked if the question should not be whether women were fit for suffrage but whether men were.*

Conservative Kentucky preachers, politicians and the press blasted Breckinridge and her fellow suffragists. Ministers sermonized that the women's rights movement was anti-Christian, claiming that God intended wives to submit to their husbands.

Some members of the Kentucky General Assembly denounced votes for women. According to *A New History of Kentucky*, a state senator declared, "Give me a wife that can love, honor, and look up to me as her lord and shield, or give me separation and death."

Henry Watterson, sharp-penned editor of the *Louisville Courier-Journal*, the state's most powerful newspaper, thundered against putting ballots into women's hands. He dismissed suffragists as "he women," "Silly-Sallies" and "Crazy Janes," Harrison and Klotter wrote.

Undaunted, Breckinridge tirelessly lobbied state lawmakers in Frankfort, urging them to support the Nineteenth Amendment. In the end, the Kentucky General Assembly endorsed the constitutional change. "In November 1920 Kentucky women voted and for the first time had equality in suffrage matters," Harrison and Klotter explained.

Madge Breckinridge cast a ballot in Lexington, but she died of another stroke soon afterward. "Her tragedy was that she voted but once," Harrison and Klotter wrote. "Her triumph was that she and others had voted, at last."

"DEAD FRED"

Fred Vinson went down in Kentucky history as the only Supreme Court chief justice from the Bluegrass State.

He is better known at Centre College, his alma mater, as "Dead Fred," the school's most faithful football fan. "He died in 1953 but hasn't missed a home game since," said Tim Ungs, formerly of Centre's communications department.

For the record, Vinson is buried in Louisa, his hometown. His portrait, affectionately dubbed "Dead Fred," goes to Centre ballgames.

"Vinson loved football passionately, so he always gets an unobstructed view," Ungs said. "His fraternity brothers see to that."

Vinson belonged to Phi Delta Theta at Centre, founded in 1819 in Danville, the Boyle County seat. He graduated in 1909 and earned a Centre law degree two years later.

Phi Delts started packing Vinson's picture to football games shortly after he died. According to the story, the tradition began when some of them were hanging around the frat house just before a game.

"Isn't it too bad that Fred won't be going to any more Centre football games?" a brother supposedly said.

"Why don't we take him?" another reputedly replied.

Everybody agreed. Somebody grabbed the portrait of Vinson off the wall, and the Phi Delts lugged the likeness to the grid match.

"'Dead Fred' is in the stands for every home game," Ungs said. "He also sometimes travels to away games when Centre faces an unusually tough opponent."

Win or lose, Vinson reportedly remains solemn as a judge. But he sheds tiny tears when Centre loses, or so it is said.

"Dead Fred" also was in the audience for the 2000 vice-presidential debate on the central Kentucky campus. T.J. Brown, a Phi Delt and Centre graduate, took "Dead Fred" on a world tour in 2003.

Brown kept a journal titled "T.J. and Fred." "They visited the Vatican, watched part of the Tour de France and ran with the bulls at Pamplona, Spain," Ungs said.

President Harry Truman named Vinson chief justice in 1946. He remained on the high court until his death at age sixty-three.

Vinson, born near Louisa, the Lawrence County seat, in 1890, had been a congressman and federal judge. A World War I veteran, he was named to a series of jobs in President Franklin D. Roosevelt's administration, according to the *Kentucky Encyclopedia*. A Democrat, Vinson was Truman's

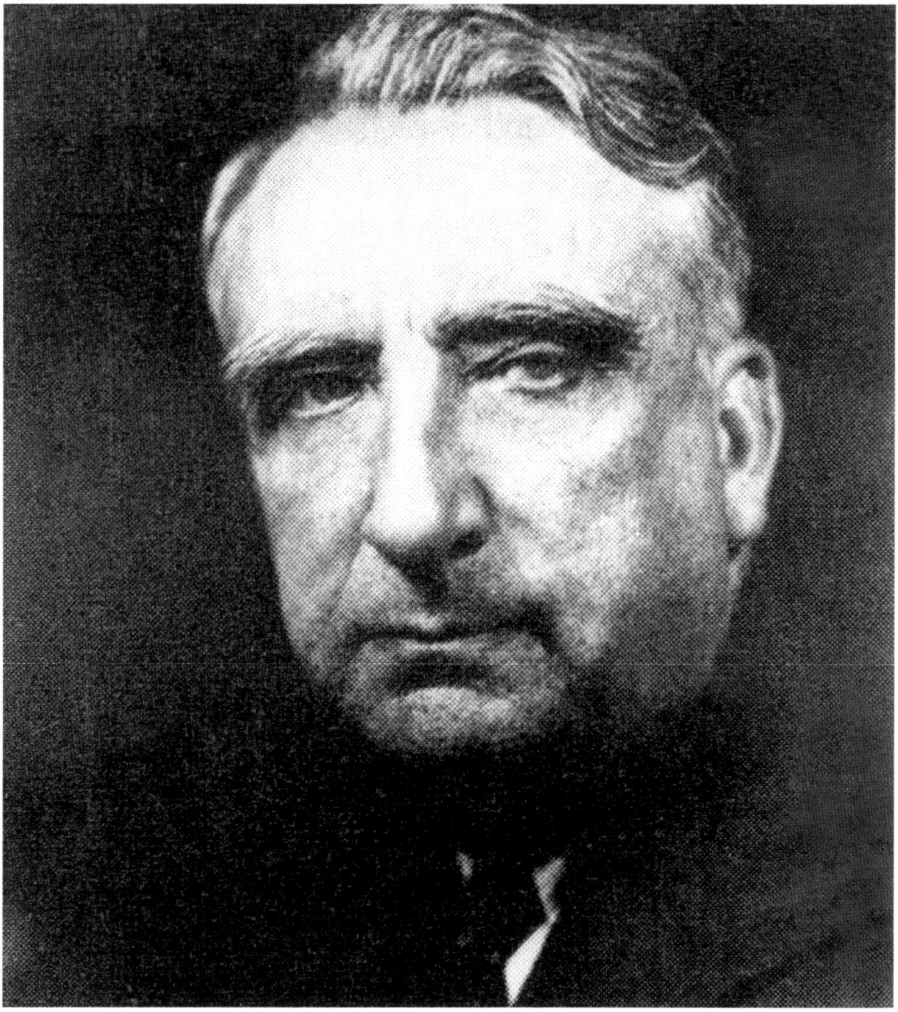

Fred M. Vinson (1890–1953). *Courtesy of the Kentucky Historical Society.*

secretary of the treasury before the president elevated him to the nation's highest court.

"Vinson was a three-sport athlete—baseball, football and basketball—who held the highest grade-point average ever achieved at Centre up to that time," Ungs said.

Chapter Four

State Solons and Others

"A Life of Intrigue"

General James H. Wilkinson doesn't fit the town-founder mold. The man who platted Frankfort, Kentucky's capital was a schemer, if not twice a traitor. "He was the sort of person who would make Benedict Arnold seem like a patriot," Harrison said.

Wilkinson Street in Kentucky's capital is named for the Maryland-born general. Nonetheless, Wilkinson was one of the most unsavory characters in Bluegrass State history, according to Harrison, a retired Western Kentucky University history professor.

Allegedly, Wilkinson plotted to pry Kentucky from the United States in 1787 and 1804. His co-conspirators supposedly were Spain and the infamous Aaron Burr.

"James Wilkinson lived a life of intrigue," wrote Harrison and Klotter in *A New History of Kentucky*. "No superior was ever safe from his machinations."

During the American Revolution, Wilkinson and some other officers tried to depose General George Washington. After the war, Wilkinson settled in Kentucky, speculated in land and landed in debt.

Wilkinson looked to Spain to bail him out. In 1787, he told the governor of Spanish New Orleans that Kentucky was close to separating from Virginia, its parent state.

Wilkinson suggested that he could deliver Kentucky to Spain if the price was right. "He wanted a trade monopoly, a royal pension, and a suitable rank and position if Kentucky became associated with Spain," Harrison and Klotter wrote.

The governor gave Wilkinson permission to sell up to $37,000 worth of produce in the Crescent City, after which the general headed home. He sailed to the East Coast, then to Kentucky aboard "a four-wheeled carriage pulled by a perfectly matched team and with black servants as outriders," according to *A New History of Kentucky*.

It is not known if Wilkinson really planned to deal Kentucky to Spain or just wanted to fatten his wallet at the expense of a gullible governor. The episode went down in history as the Spanish Conspiracy.

Meanwhile, Wilkinson laid out Frankfort, which the Virginia legislature incorporated in 1791, according to the *Kentucky Encyclopedia*. The Kentucky legislature named Frankfort the state capital in 1792.

A decade later, Wilkinson was back in hot water. After the general's old friend, Vice President Aaron Burr, shot Alexander Hamilton in a famous duel, the discredited Burr purportedly planned to carve a new nation from U.S. territory west of the Appalachian Mountains, including Kentucky, and make himself emperor.

Allegedly, Wilkinson was part of the so-called Burr Conspiracy. In 1805, he and Burr met secretly at Fort Massac on the Ohio River in southern Illinois. What plot, if any, Burr and Wilkinson hatched at the tiny frontier outpost is still a mystery.

Later, Wilkinson got cold feet and condemned Burr in a letter to President Thomas Jefferson. Burr was tried for treason and acquitted. Wilkinson was court-martialed but found innocent. He ended up in Mexico City, where he died in 1825 at age sixty-eight.

Harrison said that it is impossible to know if Frankfort's founder was a two-time traitor or was just plain greedy. "I think he played things by ear," the historian suggested. "He was always ready to take advantage of an opportunity."

"THE TRAGEDY UNPARALLELED IN KENTUCKY HISTORY"

A brawl that left both combatants dead was proposed as a reason Kentucky governors should no longer have to swear that they had never fought a duel.

Never mind that the 1889 fight in which A.M. Swope and William Cassius Goodloe killed each other was "the tragedy unparalleled in Kentucky history." Forget that the bloodshed was cited as more proof by non-Kentuckians that the Bluegrass State was a violent, lawless place to be avoided.

During the 1890–91 convention called to write a new state constitution, delegate W.G. Bullitt of Paducah argued that the Goodloe-Swope affair was "a reason to remove the provision requiring an anti-dueling oath," said Robert M. Ireland, a University of Kentucky history professor and author.

Because dueling was so common in early Kentucky, the 1850 state charter required officeholders from the governor down to promise that they had neither dueled nor acted as a second for a duelist. Bullitt argued "that the code duello actually reduced the number of honor killings because it contained a mechanism for diplomatic settlements of disputes," Ireland said.

Dueling was never legal in Kentucky. But aristocratic hotbloods went by the code duello, which "involved a formal challenge, a formal response and negotiations between the seconds that included a serious effort to settle the problem diplomatically rather than with weapons."

Ireland said that in the nineteenth century, "spontaneous, unregulated… homicidal affairs of honor" such as the Goodloe-Swope row were defined as "'defacto duels' or more often as 'street fights.' Bullitt argued that the code duello served as a way to curtail such deadly encounters."

Delegates didn't buy Bullitt's reasoning. The new constitution, approved in 1891, retained the anti-dueling oath.

Even so, the Goodloe-Swope feud was not forgotten. The fatal quarrel rated a chapter in *Famous Kentucky Tragedies and Trials*.

"The cause leading to the duel between the two men and which culminated in the tragedy unparalleled in the history of Kentucky, dated back several years," author Johnson wrote. Nonetheless, the duelists' backgrounds suggested that they should have been friends.

Swope and Goodloe were Lincoln County natives. They were Yankee officers in the Civil War and loyal Republicans in Lexington afterward. But "a feeling of political jealousy between them" grew into "bitter feeling," Johnson explained.

On November 8, 1889, Goodloe and Swope met by chance at the Lexington post office and exchanged words. Swope shot Goodloe with a pistol as Goodloe knifed him. "Goodloe…continued to plunge his dirk into the body of his adversary until he had gashed him in thirteen different places," Johnson wrote. Swope fired a second time before he fell dead.

Goodloe, though mortally wounded, managed to walk out of the post office. Passersby rushed him to a doctor's office.

Goodloe's clothes were "still burning from the effects of the powder, showing that Col. Swope's pistol must have been almost against him when the shots were fired," Johnson wrote. Transferred to a Lexington hotel, Goodloe died two days later.

The Sportsman's Hill Scalp

Did William Whitley ask his fellow Kentuckians to scalp him if he fell to the foe? The old frontiersman died in the Battle of the Thames near Fairfield, Ontario, in the War of 1812. He was sixty-four.

Supposedly, Whitley told his comrades in arms to lift his hair should British soldiers or Indian warriors kill him. "He knew his body couldn't be brought home for burial," Patty Pope said. "He thought his scalp could be. But that may be just folklore."

Pope worked at the William Whitley House State Historic Site near Stanford, seat of Lincoln County. The two-story dwelling was Kentucky's first brick house, according to Pope.

There is no record of Whitley's scalp being interred at Sportsman's Hill, the Whitley estate. "But it's a story that has been told for a long time," Pope said.

Born in Virginia, Whitley moved to Kentucky in 1775. He fought Indians during the American Revolution, and after Kentucky became a state, he served a term in the legislature.

Whitley was fiercely anti-British. When he built a racetrack near his house, he had horses run counterclockwise on clay rather than clockwise on grass, as in Britain. "To this day, all American sports using oval tracks race counterclockwise," the *Kentucky Encyclopedia* explains.

Whitley was able to soldier in his sixties because he "was a man above the ordinary size, of great muscular power, and capable of enduring great fatigue and privation," Lewis and Richard Collins note in their *History of Kentucky*.

Whitley rode with Colonel Richard M. Johnson's storied regiment of Kentucky mounted riflemen in the Battle of the Thames, fought near Fairfield, Ontario, on October 5, 1813. The battle took its name from a nearby stream named for the famous river that flows through Britain's capital.

The Americans, most of them Kentuckians, faced a force of British troops and their Native American allies. Johnson led part of his regiment against the Indians, who were hidden in a swamp. Tecumseh, the famous Shawnee chief, led the Indians.

Dubbed "the Forlorn Hope," Whitley and nineteen men volunteered to draw the Indians' fire. Johnson's main force would then quickly attack before the Indians could reload their muskets.

"Fifteen of the heroic band, including Whitley, were killed immediately," Hammack wrote. Four more were wounded; only one of the Forlorn Hope escaped unscathed, the author added.

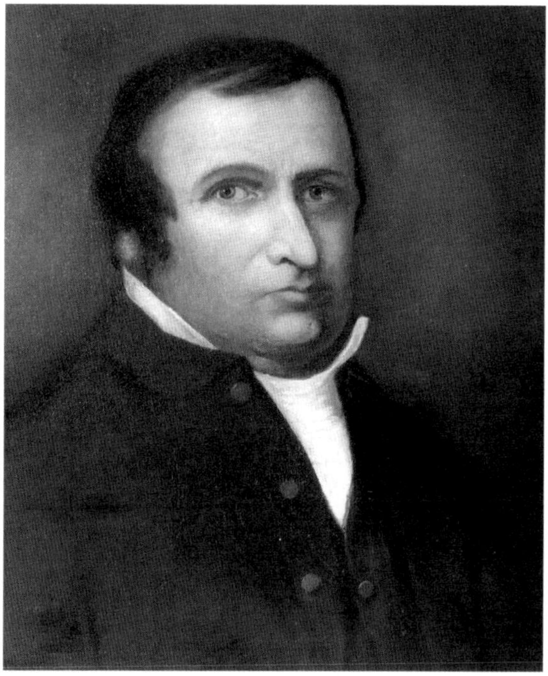

William Whitley (1749–1813). *Courtesy of the Kentucky Historical Society.*

Whitley reportedly was buried where he fell. The grave is unmarked.

Part of the battlefield is preserved in a small roadside park that features a stone memorial to Tecumseh. The chief perished in the battle, a victory for the Americans.

"According to other legends, Whitley killed Tecumseh or Tecumseh killed Whitley," Pope said. "We don't have any proof of that either."

Johnson, from Scott County, was credited with slaying Tecumseh. He was elected U.S. vice president in 1836 on the slogan, "Rumpsey Dumpsey, Rumpsey Dumpsey, Colonel Johnson killed Tecumseh."

Whitley was not forgotten. "Whitley County, Kentucky, and Whitley County, Indiana, are named for him," Pope said.

"Who Is George Shannon?"

"Peg Leg" Shannon slipped through the cracks of Kentucky history. The youngest member of the famous Lewis and Clark Expedition became a controversial, headline-grabbing, one-legged Kentucky judge. He was also a lawyer and lawmaker in the Bluegrass State and in Missouri, where Shannon County was named for him.

"He is not very well known in Kentucky," Bryant said. "We don't have much information about him."

Even so, Captain William Clark remembered Shannon as "one of the most active and useful men we had." He named a western wilderness stream for the teenager Captain Meriwether Lewis recruited from Maysville, Kentucky.

"George [his real name] Shannon became the most educated, the most accomplished, and even the most colorful" of the Kentucky volunteers with Lewis and Clark, explained archivist Carolyn S. Denton of Palm Beach, Florida, in *Nine Young Men From Kentucky*. Mostly written by Louisville historian George H. Yater, the little book is about the Kentuckians with Lewis and Clark.

The expedition began in 1804, lasted until 1806 and covered eight thousand miles from St. Louis to the Pacific Ocean and back. Lewis and Clark led approximately forty explorers through the new Louisiana Purchase and beyond.

In 1807, Clark hired Shannon as an "Indian conductor" to escort a Mandan chief from St. Charles, Missouri, near St. Louis, to his home sixteen hundred miles back up the Missouri River. In North Dakota, Arikara Indians attacked the Shannon party. Shannon was shot in the leg, although records do not say which one.

The nearest doctor was in St. Charles. Shannon's wound was field dressed, but gangrene set in on the return trip. Amputation seemed inevitable, although one source claimed, "Had he taken care of himself...the limb would have been saved, but he ventured to walk upon it before it was entirely well, and broke off the bone afresh."

A St. Charles surgeon removed the leg above the knee. Shannon nearly died and needed almost a year to recover in an army hospital, according to Denton, a Kentucky native and former archivist at Transylvania University in Lexington. "He used a wooden peg for the rest of his life, which earned him the nickname 'Peg Leg,'" she wrote.

Despite his disability, Shannon was fit enough to explore saltpeter caves in Missouri with Lewis. But in 1808, the youngster returned to Kentucky for an education. He enrolled at Transylvania, apparently to study law. Two years later, he left for Philadelphia to help Nicholas Biddle edit *The Journals of Lewis and Clark*.

Clark wrote Biddle on behalf of Shannon, who was an expert on Native American sign language. The youth "possesses a sincere and undisguised heart, he is highly spoken of by all his acquaintances and much respected at the Lexington University where he has been for the past two years," Clark explained. "Since the misfortune of loseing [*sic*] his leg, he has been studiously employed in persute [*sic*] of an education...He wishes to study Law and practice in the Western Country."

Shannon came back to Lexington in 1812, became an attorney and got married. He hobnobbed with local leaders, including Henry Clay, who would become Kentucky's greatest statesman.

Shannon was appointed messenger for the Kentucky electors in the presidential election of 1812, in which James Madison carried the Bluegrass State en route to capturing the White House. Afterward, a Madison supporter in Kentucky commended Shannon to the president as "the young man that lost his leg in the Battle with the Indians in taking home the Osage [*sic*] Indian Chife [*sic*] and also was in the Expedition with Lewis and Clark to the Pacific Ocean." The Madison booster also said Shannon "intends to petition for some compensation, in consequence of his being disabled."

Shannon's law practice prospered and grew with Lexington. The citizens elected him to the state House of Representatives, and he served from 1820 to 1823.

Apparently, Shannon was not above reproach. "Once he entered public life, his character was questioned on several occasions in the local papers and in handbills," Denton wrote.

"Who is George Shannon?" an opponent's flier challenged in 1824, when the lawmaker sought another term. "What are his private and moral virtues, and what is his public and political character?"

The handbill listed several reasons why Shannon shouldn't be voted back to the legislature. He wasn't, but the balloting was close.

In 1824, Governor Joseph Desha named his friend Shannon a circuit judge. The next year, "Peg Leg" became embroiled in one of the most famous scandals in nineteenth-century Kentucky. Shannon presided over the sensational murder and robbery trial of Isaac Desha, the governor's son, in Cynthiana, the Harrison County seat. Shannon and the governor were friends and political allies.

The jury found young Desha guilty and sentenced him to hang. Shannon overturned the verdict and ordered a new trial, claiming that the evidence didn't support the jury's decision.

Anti-Desha politicians and publishers charged political favoritism and angrily demanded Shannon's removal from the bench. "According to a Frankfort newspaper, George was burned in effigy in both Harrison and Bourbon counties," Denton wrote.

Evidently to beat the political heat, Shannon migrated to Missouri. Despite the judge's tarnished reputation in Kentucky, President Andrew Jackson appointed him a U.S. attorney for the Show Me State in 1830.

Shannon also served in the Missouri House and Senate before he died in Palmyra, Missouri, near St. Charles, in 1836. He was forty-nine.

According to a St. Louis newspaper, Shannon's funeral was attended by "a large assemblage of the ladies and gentlemen" of Palmyra, who tendered "their last testimony of respect to the remains of a good man." Denton wrote that lawyers in Palmyra and St. Charles wore black armbands for thirty days. Shannon's fellow attorneys, she added, published resolutions "that to the genius, learning and eloquence which rendered him a shining member of the legal profession, he added those social qualities which rendered him a pleasant and agreeable companion."

Despite such high praise, there are no monuments to Peg Leg Shannon in Missouri or Kentucky. Shannon is buried in an unmarked grave in a little cemetery near Palmyra, Denton said. The tiny tributary of the Yellowstone River that Clark named for Shannon is now known as Sand Creek.

Purportedly, the "pleasant and agreeable" Shannon was fond of gambling and strong drink. Denton quoted an old Missouri history book in which the author cited a novel proposition put to "Peg Leg" and a compatriot by a third party. Apparently, all three men were drunk in a tavern.

"If either would do a particular act, and the other should fail to follow suit, the delinquent should treat the crowd," the author wrote. "Thereupon Shannon took off his wooden leg and threw it into the fire; and as the other one was not disposed to thus jeopardize a sound limb, he was forced to foot the bill."

"SAFE FROM ALL THEIR CRUEL FOES"

The long poem on Jereboam and Ann Cook Beauchamp's tombstone in Bloomfield is supposed to tell a tragic tale of true love:

Entomb'd within each other's arms
The husband and the wife repose,
Safe from life's never-ending storms,
And safe from all their cruel foes.

Some say Jereboam and Ann, husband and wife, were Kentucky's version of Romeo and Juliet. Others claim that he was a coldblooded killer or a love-struck dupe, whom a scheming Ann goaded into murder.

The couple died tragically. Ann—sometimes called Anna—killed herself as Jereboam was hanged.

The Beauchamps' final resting place is the best-known grave in Maple Grove Cemetery in Bloomfield, Kentucky. But their story is known far beyond where they sleep eternally.

"It has such drama and such tragedy, that lots of people have written about it," Bryant said.

Edgar Allan Poe fictionalized the short, unhappy lives of Jereboam and Ann. So did Kentucky-born author Robert Penn Warren in his novel *World Enough and Time*.

The real story began on state representative Solomon Sharp's Frankfort doorstep. A pounding on the door woke him up at 2:00 a.m. on November 7, 1825.

When Sharp opened the door, a man pulled a knife and stabbed him in the chest. Sharp, thirty-eight, fell dead in a pool of blood. The assailant fled into the darkness, according to the *Kentucky Encylopedia.*

Sharp was a veteran politician, having also served as a congressman and state attorney general. But he had enemies, none worse than John V. Waring.

When Sharp ran for the legislature in 1824, Waring circulated handbills accusing Sharp of seducing Ann Cook and fathering her illegitimate child, who was born in 1820, the encylopedia says.

Sharp won anyway, but Waring remained his foe. At first, authorities investigated Waring. But he had an ironclad alibi. So did Patrick Darby, another suspect.

Meanwhile, the legislature tried to help find Sharp's killer. Lawmakers offered a $3,000 reward for the arrest and conviction of Sharpe's killer.

Ultimately, suspicion shifted to Jereboam Beauchamp, a twenty-three-year-old law student who had married Ann in 1824. The couple lived in Bowling Green, about 120 miles from Frankfort.

Beauchamp had both motive and opportunity. After Waring put out the handbills, Ann, fifteen years her husband's senior, allegedly confessed to Jereboam that Sharp was a libertine and the father of her child. Supposedly, she encouraged Jereboam to kill Sharp.

In any event, Beauchamp was in Frankfort on the night of the Sharp murder. Believing that the youth killed Sharp, law officers arrested him in Bowling Green. He went on trial in Frankfort on May 8, 1826.

Beauchamp admitted to slaying Sharp. He said it was a crime of passion to avenge his wife's honor.

Nonetheless, the judge sentenced Beauchamp to hang in the capital city on July 7, 1826. In the meantime, the condemned man awaited execution in the state prison.

Ann persuaded prison authorities to let her stay with Jereboam until his day of doom. Ann moved into her husband's tiny cell.

Secretly, the couple plotted to cheat the hangman. They would kill themselves.

They tried on July 5. The couple swallowed what they thought was a lethal dose of laudanum, a powerful painkiller made from opium. Somehow, Jereboam and Ann survived.

Afterward, a guard stayed with them in the cell. But on the morning Jereboam was to die, Ann asked the guard to leave while she got dressed.

When the guard exited, Ann produced a smuggled knife. She stabbed herself and collapsed. Jereboam grabbed the knife and stabbed himself. According to historian J. Winston Coleman's book *The Beauchamp-Sharp Tragedy*, Jereboam, still conscious when the guard returned, pleaded with him to "tell my father that my wife and myself are going straight to heaven. We are dying."

The guard helped rush Ann to the nearby jailer's house. A doctor worked frantically to save Ann's life.

Prison guards hustled the badly wounded Jereboam to the gallows before he could die by his own hand, according to the *Kentucky Encyclopedia*. "When he proved too weak to stand, he was supported by two men as the rope was placed around his neck," the encyclopedia added. In yet another bizarre twist to the story, Jereboam had hired a band to play "Bonaparte's Retreat" as he was put to death.

While their suicide pact failed, Ann and Jereboam died simultaneously. Almost at the instant her husband was hanged, Ann's life ebbed away, too.

Beauchamp's father lived in Bloomfield, about forty miles from Frankfort. He claimed the bodies of his son and daughter-in-law and arranged for Jereboam and Ann to be put in a large coffin together. Jereboam's right arm was draped around Ann's neck, Coleman wrote.

Reunited in death, Jereboam and Ann were buried on Bloomfield's grassy cemetery hill. Ann wrote the poem that was their epitaph. The verses were chiseled on a white marble slab that covers the grave.

Time and the elements have not been kind to the slab, which is weatherworn and cracked in five places. Grass stubbornly sprouts through the fissures, making the poem hard to read.

But somebody erected a newer gray granite tombstone. It is inscribed with the old poem, which ends:

His wife disdain'd a life forlorn,
Without her heart's lov'd, honour'd lord;

Then, reader, hear thy fortunes mourn,
Who for their love, their life-blood pour'd.

In *Kentucky: Land of Contrast*, Clark wrote that Robert Penn Warren clothed Jereboam and Ann "in robes of a kind of Kentucky chivalry and gallantry." The poem-epitaph, he added, "ensures romantic interest in the tragedy."

Coleman saw nothing romantic about the death of Sharp. He claimed Beauchamp was a coldblooded killer, describing him as "satanic."

"The Blood of These Hessians Would Poison the Most Degraded Tumble Bug in Creation"

Yankees weren't just the enemy to Len G. Faxon, Civil War editor of the *Columbus Crescent*. They were "bow-legged, wooden-shoed, sour craut stinking, Bologna sausage eating, hen roost robbing Dutch sons of ---." Their commander was a thieving, lying lush who "embodied the leprous rascalities of the world" and deserved to be hanged.

Objectivity was not a hallmark of Civil War journalism. America's bloodiest conflict was a mother lode of media bias. Vitriol and vilification were the stock-in-trade of editors, North and South. But few verbal broadsides were as withering as Faxon's 1861 *Crescent* blast. It even amazed the "world's first and greatest" war correspondent, Sir William Howard Russell of the *London Times*. Russell preserved Faxon's fulminations in *My Diary North and South*, his American Civil War journal.

Faxon might have been Kentucky's most Southern-sympathizing editor, but there is no doubt that he spoke for most of his readers. Few Kentucky towns were more pro-Confederate than Columbus, a busy little Mississippi river port and railhead of about one thousand inhabitants in 1861, the first year of the Civil War.

Shortly after the war started, Union forces occupied Cairo, Illinois, at the confluence of the Mississippi and Ohio Rivers about fifteen miles from Columbus.

Kentucky declared itself neutral, a stance that failed to stop Columbus from showing its true colors. In June, with several local men already away in the Confederate army, pro-Southern citizens hoisted a big Rebel Stars and Bars over the town.

Even before, Columbus's sympathies were hardly a secret to the Yankees at Cairo. The post commander, Colonel Benjamin Prentiss, suspected that citizens of Columbus were spying on his troops and trading with the

Confederate enemy. But checked by Kentucky neutrality, Prentiss kept his soldiers away from Columbus.

Still, he kept a wary eye on the port town with its one-hundred-foot dirt bluffs from which an army could command the river for miles around. Prentiss also knew that Confederate troops were poised at Union City, Tennessee, only thirty miles south of Columbus.

Therefore, Prentiss regularly sent boats to patrol the Mississippi and Ohio. On June 12, 1861, he ordered the steamer *City of Alton*, with a small group of infantry aboard, to scout the Mississippi as far as Columbus. Just in case there was trouble, he had the little paddle-wheeler armed with a field gun or two.

The boatload of bluecoats spotted no Rebels. But Yankee hackles rose when the soldiers spied Columbus's Confederate flag. The *City of Alton* chugged toward the town landing.

Down clattered the wooden gangplank. Musket-toting Union troops scrambled ashore, led by Colonel Dick Oglesby, an Illinoisan who would become a general, governor and United States senator. The Northern soldiers eagerly tore down the enemy banner, claiming themselves a war trophy.

Pro-Southern Columbus citizens shot only dirty looks at the unwelcome visitors. But a man defiantly told the *Alton*'s skipper that "Columbus is all right for the South." A plucky, patriotic woman promised that "she had enough material to make another flag of the same description, and that it would be flying before sundown."

It is unknown if Len G. Faxon witnessed the flagnapping. But after the Yankees were gone, he opened fire in the *Crescent*.

Had it not been for Russell, Faxon's fusillade might have been forgotten. No copies of the 1861 *Crescent* are known to survive. Russell, who had reported on the Indian mutiny and the Crimean War, was in the Union camp at Cairo when he read the *Crescent* with Faxon's version of the flag snatching.

Russell quoted Faxon's wish that the folds of the flag "had contained a thousand asps to sting a thousand Dutchmen to eternity unshriven." The Yankees probably would have been too beery to feel it, according to the editor. "The mosquitoes of Cairo have been sucking the lager-bier out of the dirty soldiers up there so long, they are bloated and swelled up as large as spring 'possums," he wrote.

> *An assortment of Columbus mosquitoes went up there the other day to suck some, but as they have not returned, the probability is that they went off with delirium tremens; in fact the blood of these Hessians would poison the most degraded tumble bug in creation.*

With that, Faxon reloaded and fired again:

> *When the bow-legged, wooden-shoed, sour craut stinking, Bologna sausage eating, hen roost robbing Dutch sons of --- had accomplished the brilliant feat of taking down the Secession flag on the river bank, they were pointed to another flag of the same sort which their guns did not cover, flying gloriously and defiantly, and dared yea! double big black dog-dared, as we used to say at school, to take that flag down.*

The bluecoats declined, Faxon claimed. "The cowardly pups, the thieving sheep dogs, the sneaking skunks dared not do so, because their twelve pieces of artillery were not bearing on it."

After flaying the Federal soldiers, Faxon lambasted their leader Prentiss, a tough as boot leather soldier who would make general and become a Union hero at the Battle of Shiloh in April 1862. Faxon dismissed him as

> *a miserable hound, a dirty dog, a sociable fellow, a treacherous villain, a notorious thief, a lying blackguard, who has served his regular five years in the penitentiary and keeps his hide continually full of Cincinnati whiskey—in him are embodied the leprous rascalities of the world, and in this living score, the gallows is cheated of its own.*

Finally, Faxon tossed down the gauntlet: "Prentiss wants our scalps: we propose a plan by which he may get that valuable article." The colonel could choose 150 of his best fighters "or 250 of his lager-bier Dutchmen." Faxon would find 100 Columbus worthies as challengers. "Then let both parties meet where there will be no interruption at the scalping business and the longest pole will knock the persimmon," Faxon vowed. "If he does not accept this proposal, he is a coward."

Prentiss ignored Faxon. But Russell suspected that Prentiss was more wounded by the editor's poison pen than the colonel admitted.

In the fall of 1861, Faxon swapped his pen for a sword. The editor gave up the *Crescent* to raise a company of guerrilla scouts for the Confederate army. He evidently survived the war but never returned to Columbus.

Faxon left Columbus about the time most of his fellow citizens welcomed the Confederate army to town "with the liveliest delight." Commanded by General Leonidas Polk, the Rebels got busy digging deep trenches on the rusty, iron ore–streaked town bluffs, which the French explorers Marquette and Joliet had named the Iron Banks two centuries before. Locals thrilled at the sight of long-range cannons with menacing monikers like "Soul

Searcher," "Snorter," "Yankee Smolluxer," "Rib Smasher," "Cunning Cuss" and "Lady Polk," the latter named in honor of the general's wife.

The Confederates also stretched a mile-long chain across the river to block Yankee gunboats. A few links and a forty-two-hundred-pound warship anchor used to fasten the chain to the Kentucky shore are featured attractions at Columbus-Belmont State Park.

Nobody was happier with the Rebels' arrival than Edward I. Bullock, the *Crescent*'s new editor. Dropping all pretense of journalistic independence, he renamed the paper the *Confederate News* and nearly equaled Faxon at bluecoat baiting:

> *We want to kill a Yankee...must kill a Yankee...never can sleep sound again until we do kill a Yankee, get his overcoat and scalp. Indian-like we want a scalp and must have it...We'd think no more of scalping a dead Yank than we would of cutting the throat of a midnight assassin...not a shade's difference between the murderer and the deceptious Yank.*

Bullock never got a Yankee scalp. He fled Columbus with the outflanked Rebel army in March 1862. The Confederates abandoned their Gibraltar after Forts Henry and Donelson in Tennessee fell to a combined Union army–navy force under General Ulysses S. Grant in February. In November 1861, Grant had led a small Union force against Belmont, Missouri, opposite Columbus, but he retreated.

Bullock ended up safely behind Confederate lines at Richmond, Virginia, the Rebel capital. He returned to Columbus in 1864 but apparently didn't give the town's Yankee occupiers any trouble. Even so, he must have been mortified to see the *Crescent* turned *Confederate News* become the *War Eagle*. "Edited and Published by Sergt. H.L. Goodall, Co. 'D' 2d Ill. Cav. Government Printer," the masthead proclaimed, according to Hall Allen.

"The Issue Is...Whether the Law Is to Be Defied or Obeyed"

Richard Reid's epitaph only hints at the bizarre tragedy that drove him to suicide 120 years ago. "Martyr to law," it reads in part.

Buried in Mount Sterling, his hometown, the Superior Court judge shot himself in 1884 after local attorney John Jay Cornelison savagely caned and whipped him in public. Reid refused to fight back on principle.

"He desired vindication from the people. Instead, he discovered devastating disapproval," wrote Klotter in *Kentucky Justice, Southern Honor, and American Manhood: Understanding the Life and Death of Richard Reid.*

Many of the gentle judge's fellow citizens shunned him as a coward. A candidate for the Court of Appeals when he turned the other cheek, Reid probably would have lost the election had he lived, according to Klotter.

The attack on Reid, followed by his depression and death, made headlines nationwide. The episode helped fuel Kentucky's reputation as a violent and lawless place, said Klotter, who doesn't believe the judge was craven. "He refused to let his society's cultural call for blood sway his beliefs," the historian said.

Yet the old notion of an eye for an eye survives in the Bluegrass State, Klotter acknowledged. "One individual said to me, after reading the book, that he didn't see how Reid could not have fought back and killed Cornelison."

Cornelison bloodied Reid with a hickory cane and a cowhide whip, bragging that he struck the judge "twenty-five times with his cane and seventy-five or a hundred times more with the whip as he chased him a block and a half," Klotter wrote.

Cornelison said he thrashed "the d----d rascal" for wronging him in a legal matter. Reid denied the charge. He also said that as a judge, he was duty bound not to strike Cornelison. Reid argued:

> *The issue is...whether the law is to be defied or obeyed, whether a judicial officer should be required to avenge a wrong done him, by taking summary vengeance in his own hands, or is to be commended for forbearing to resort to violence and for upholding the majesty of law.*

Some Kentuckians sided with Reid. The *Louisville Courier-Journal*, the state's largest paper, called the embattled judge's conduct "manly," according to Klotter's book.

Others, including the editor of the *Hickman Courier*, found it "difficult to understand how any self-respecting citizen can submit to such punishment." Self-defense, "to say nothing of true manhood," demanded retaliation, the editor added.

Cornelison was found guilty of assault and battery and sentenced to three years in jail. He appealed, ultimately lost and wound up behind bars in 1887. But in 1888, Governor Simon Bolivar Buckner, an ex–Confederate general, pardoned Cornelison.

A bronze statue of Richard Reid towers over his grave in the cemetery at Mount Sterling. "Whether by design or not, the statue…has its back to the town that he believed had turned its back on his cause," Klotter wrote.

"A Spirit Lamp, a Small Skillet, Some Bacon and Eggs"

Did the sweet scent of sizzling bacon create Carlisle County? On April 3, 1886, Speaker Charles Offutt of Bourbon County purportedly promised not to adjourn the Kentucky House of Representatives for lunch until lawmakers voted on a measure to make Carlisle the Bluegrass State's 119th county.

There was opposition. One solon in particular questioned the creation of yet another small county.

Meanwhile, midday mealtime came and went. Offutt started frying bacon on a portable stove.

"The aroma…permeated the room [and]…it made every man present hungry," wrote Ran Graves in his *History and Memories of Carlisle County*. The naysayer to the new county, "being used to eating his biggest meal at noon…submitted gracefully," the author added.

The House voted Carlisle into the commonwealth. Offutt dismissed legislators for a late lunch.

The story seems all but forgotten in Carlisle County, about as far west as Kentucky goes. "I'd venture to say that 99.9 percent of the people have never heard it," said Larry Kelley, a founder of the Ballard-Carlisle County Historical and Genealogical Society.

Kelley lives in Carlisle County, whose seat is Bardwell. He runs radio station WGKY in Wickliffe, seat of Ballard County. With Senate concurrence, the General Assembly carved Carlisle County from south Ballard County. Both counties are next to the Mississippi River.

Southern Ballard Countians had sought a county of their own. Mayfield Creek, which split Ballard County, often flooded. Citizens complained that high water made it hard to get to the county seat, then at Blandville, north of the stream that empties into the Mississippi.

Representative Thomas Turk Gardner of Ballard County supported the Carlisle County bill, which "encountered stubborn resistance from some of the members of the Legislature," Graves wrote. "They used delaying tactics and wouldn't let the bill come to a vote."

Lieutenant Governor John G. Carlisle, for whom the new county was to be named, backed the bill. So did "quite a block of men" including Representative William P. Thorne of Henry County, Gardner's chief ally.

"T.T. Gardner buttonholed the speaker on [the] morning [of April 3]," Graves wrote. Offutt instructed Gardner to have Thorne read the Carlisle "bill between eleven and twelve o'clock and he would not let the Legislature adjourn until they had voted either for or against the bill."

One by one, foes of the measure called for adjournment. Offutt ruled them out of order, according to Graves.

At 2:00 p.m., Offutt dispatched a page to fetch "a spirit lamp, a small skillet, some bacon and eggs," Graves wrote. The frying bacon cooked the opposition.

When south Ballard dwellers heard that the Carlisle County bill passed, "there was great rejoicing," Graves wrote. "They made big bonfires that night, shooting cannons, firecrackers, and exploding a charge of powder between two anvils which made an explosion equal to a small cannon."

"Each of Them Knew that the Other Was Dead Game"

Charles Julian went to the Capital Hotel in Frankfort to buy a ticket for Senator William Jennings Bryan's speech. He ended up dead, caught in the crossfire of a 1900 shootout between an ex-member of Congress and a former governor's nephew that apparently spilled more innocent blood than any affair of honor in Kentucky history.

Besides Julian, the row claimed the life of gunman Ethelbert D. Scott of Somerset and another bystander. Four others were hurt.

Former U.S. Representative David Colson, a Middlesboro Republican, slew Scott, whose uncle was William O. Bradley, Kentucky's first Republican governor. Scott, thirty, wounded Colson, thirty-seven.

The Capital Hotel is gone. The gunfight doesn't rate much ink in history books. "It definitely was overshadowed by the Goebel assassination," Bryant said.

Colson and Scott shot it out on January 16, 1900. Two weeks later, an unknown sniper mortally wounded Democrat William Goebel, the only American governor ever assassinated in office.

Though Colson and Scott were Republicans, they were bitter enemies from the Spanish-American War. Neither one saw combat, but they fought each other with revolvers. A groin wound left Colson partly paralyzed.

Colson and Scott came to Frankfort to support Republican William S. Taylor after the close and hotly disputed governor's election of 1899. A special commission said that Taylor won. The legislature named Goebel governor.

Scott and Colson each claimed to his friends that "the other was pursuing him," Johnson wrote in *Famous Kentucky Tragedies and Trials*. It was just after noon when Colson and Scott spied each other at the hotel. "Each of them knew that the other was dead game and that one or both of them must die," the author added.

Hotel guests dove for cover when the enemies pulled pistols. Colson claimed Scott fired first, but "the question as to which of them fired the first shot has never been settled," Johnson wrote. In less than a minute, Colson emptied two six-shooters and Scott one.

Scott grabbed Luther W. Demaree of Shelbyville as a human shield. Colson, allegedly blinded by gun smoke, fired three times, killing Demaree, Johnson wrote.

A stray bullet struck the leg of Julian, who farmed near Frankfort. "The poor man was in the hotel lobby to buy a ticket for the Bryan speech that evening," said Bryant. Julian bled to death in twenty minutes, Johnson wrote.

Other errant rounds hit Harry McEwan of Louisville in the foot and Ben Golden of Barboursville in the back. Golden allegedly came to the hotel with Scott.

When the shooting started, C.D. Redpath, a traveling salesman from Chicago, jumped off the shoeshine stand and fell into the basement stairwell. He broke his leg.

Meanwhile, Colson wounded Scott twice in the abdomen and once in the neck. Scott shot Colson in the arm. Out of bullets, he fled for the basement with Colson in pursuit.

When Scott reached the top of the steps, Colson used a second pistol to shoot him in the head. Scott tumbled down the stairway and landed on Redpath.

Before he left the hotel and surrendered to the Frankfort chief of police, Colson pumped three more rounds into Scott, the last one "after he fell across Redpath," Johnson wrote.

A jury acquitted Colson for Scott's slaying, agreeing that it was self-defense. He was not tried for the deaths of Demaree or Julian. Colson, who served in Congress from 1895 to 1899, died in 1904 at age forty-three, his life evidently cut short by his first gunfight with Scott.

Cash Clay Was a Two-Gun Editor

Many an old-time Kentucky publisher packed a pistol for protection. Cassius Marcellus Clay opted for artillery. "He had two little cannons inside his newspaper office that were aimed at the door," said Lashe Mullins. "He never did fire them, though."

In 1845, "Cash" Clay started the *True American*, a fiercely antislavery newspaper in strongly proslavery Lexington. Expecting trouble, he made his office a mini-fortress, according to Mullins, curator at White Hall, Clay's mansion, which is preserved as a state historic site near Richmond.

One of Clay's old cannons is on display at 1860s-vintage White Hall.

"Unfortunately, we don't know what happened to the other one," Mullins said.

Both cannons were supposed to protect the *True American* against proslavery mobs. Probably no Kentucky publisher was more hated than Clay, whom one slavery supporter reviled as "meaner than the autocrats of hell," according to *Cassius Marcellus Clay: Firebrand of Freedom* by H. Edward Richardson.

"The hemp is ready for your neck," Clay's detractor added in a letter to the editor. "Your life cannot be spared. Plenty thirst for your blood—are determined to have it."

Clay seemed an unlikely foe of human bondage. Many members of his family, including his famous cousin, Henry Clay, owned slaves.

Cassius turned against slavery in 1832 when he was a student at Yale University. A speech by abolitionist William Lloyd Garrison converted the twenty-two-year-old Kentuckian to the emancipation cause.

Back in Kentucky, Clay's antislavery views almost cost him his life. In 1841, he survived a duel. Two years later, a proslavery assassin nearly killed him.

Undaunted, Clay began printing the *True American* in 1845. He chose "God and Liberty!" as the paper's motto, Richardson wrote.

Clay housed his newspaper in a three-story red brick building on Mill Street that he converted into a citadel. The publisher plated the shutters and doors with iron to thwart firebombers. He armed himself with muskets, lances and a pair of brass, four-pounder cannons he bought in Cincinnati.

Clay mounted the mini-guns on a breast-high table, loaded the ordnance with powder, shot and nails and trained the ordnance on the front door. Anybody who tried to silence the *True American* would pay a steep price in blood, or so the publisher planned.

In his *Memoirs*, Clay said that he recruited "six or eight persons" to defend him.

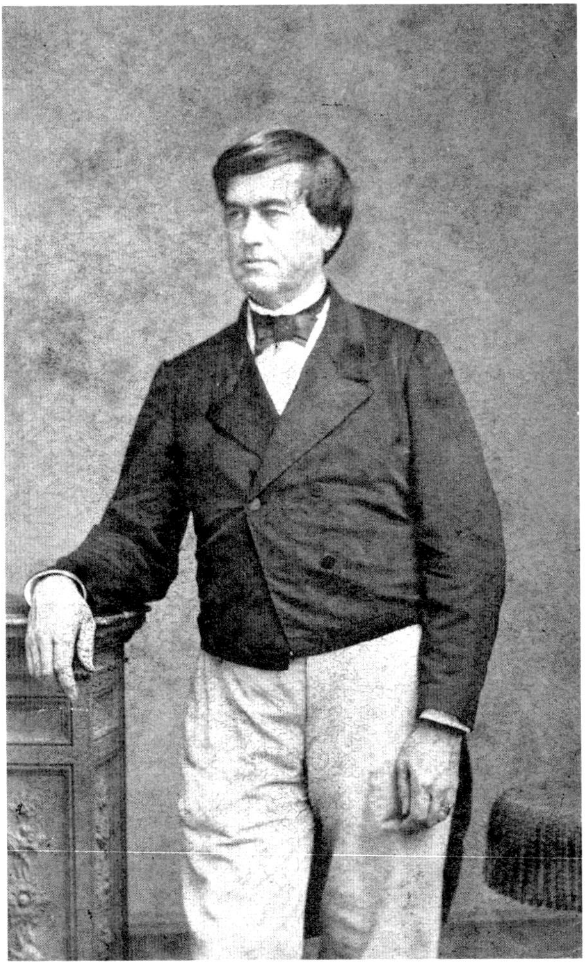

Cassius M. Clay (1810–1903). *Courtesy of the Kentucky Historical Society.*

> *If defeated, they were to escape by a trap-door in the roof; and I had placed a keg of powder, with a match, which I could set off, and blow up the office and all my invaders; and this I should most certainly have done, in case of the last extremity.*

Clay's enemies didn't strike until he was home in bed with typhoid fever. On August 18, 1845, a posse led by James B. Clay, Henry Clay's son, seized the *True American* office without opposition.

The lawmen boxed up Clay's equipment and sent it to Cincinnati, where he published the *True American* before volunteering as a captain in the Mexican War. He returned to Lexington in 1847 and continued to denounce slavery.

Clay joined the antislavery Republican party, befriended Abraham Lincoln and supported him for president in 1860. During the Civil War, Clay served as a major general and U.S. ambassador to Russia.

Clay courted controversy long after slavery was gone. He divorced his wife of forty-five years and at age eighty-four married a teenager. He lived another ten years, dying in bed—some said symbolically—as a violent thunderstorm swirled around White Hall and a lightning bolt knocked the head off Henry Clay's tall stone statue in nearby Lexington.

Mullins said that the cannon, which weighs about fifty pounds, squats on a third-floor table at White Hall, whose collection of relics includes some of Clay's pistols and Bowie knives.

Visitors are seldom taken aback by the cannon, according to Mullins. "By the time they get to the third floor, they've already learned enough about Cassius Marcellus Clay that seeing a cannon in his house wouldn't surprise them."

The "Lion of White Hall"

Did the old "Lion of White Hall" just want to prove he could still roar? In 1894, Cassius Marcellus Clay, the famous Kentucky emancipationist, took a new wife. He was eighty-four. She was about fifteen.

"In his time, young women frequently married older men," Klotter said. "Even so, the differences in their ages created a great deal of controversy."

Clay fueled the scandal by allegedly chasing a posse away with an ancient cannon. The only casualty was a maple tree, which was already dead, according to Richardson's book.

Clay and Dora Richardson, an orphan, tied the knot at White Hall, his family home near Richmond, the Madison County seat. The forty-four-room, red brick mansion built in 1799 is preserved as the White Hall State Historic Site.

Clay was born at White Hall in 1810. His fierce opposition to slavery in slave state Kentucky earned him the nickname "the Lion of White Hall."

In the 1830s, Clay's antislavery views ended his political career after just two terms in the state House of Representatives. They nearly cost him his life, too. Clay survived a duel and an assassination attempt. Undaunted, he started the *True American*, an antislavery newspaper in Lexington, which a mob suppressed.

Clay again raised eyebrows when he divorced his wife of forty-five years in 1878. He "created a local and national sensation" when he and Dora were wed sixteen years later, according to Richardson, apparently no relation to the second Mrs. Clay.

Clay's family tried to nix the nuptials but to no avail. Friends warned Clay that the union riled "self-appointed guardians of the public morals in Richmond," Richardson wrote. Sheriff Josiah P. Simmons and seven deputies reputedly rode out to White Hall to rescue Dora.

What happened next, Richardson wrote, "has passed into a kind of twilight world between fact and fantasy."

Clay had saved at least one of the two small cannons he had bought to defend the *True American* against slavery-supporting Lexingtonians. He carefully loaded one "with grapeshot mixed with nails and tacks, chiseled pieces of harrow spikes, jagged horseshoes, cut sections of trace chains, grated lead, and an assortment of nuts and bolts," Richardson wrote.

He purportedly pointed the gun "at a huge dead water maple" in front of White Hall, the author added. Supposedly, the deputies spied the cannon and took cover behind the lifeless tree while Simmons ordered Clay to surrender his spouse. Dora yelled from a window that she aimed to stay.

"With that warning, shots began to ring out," Richardson wrote. Clay reportedly replied with a cannon blast that "shattered the dead limbs of the water maple into splinters."

The tree is long gone. One of the little brass-barreled cannons is a featured attraction at White Hall.

Clay's shot supposedly ended the standoff. The octet of lawmen, Richardson added, "retrieved their frightened horses and beat a hasty retreat…"

Clay divorced Dora after about two years, Richardson added. He died in 1903 at age ninety-two and was buried in Richmond Cemetery.

"In modern day terms, we would probably look at Clay's marriage as child abuse," said Klotter. "But in analyzing the marriage, it might have been a case of an aging man's need to show his masculinity. It might have been the old lion's last roar."

"ALL I WANT TO BE IS JAILER OF LETCHER COUNTY"

It might be Kentucky's most famous political yarn. Teddy Roosevelt leads the Rough Riders to victory at San Juan Hill. No sooner do the guns fall silent than he cuts a deal with a potential rival for the presidency, Corporal Fess Whitaker of Letcher County.

"This is going to make one of us president one day," Teddy tells Fess. The teenage trooper agrees and then concedes the White House to his colonel.

"All I want to be is jailer of Letcher County," Fess demurs.

A Republican, Whitaker was elected jailer and judge of Letcher County, nearly as far east as Kentucky goes. He told and retold the Teddy Roosevelt tale on the stump in Whitesburg, the county seat, and elsewhere Letcher voters gathered.

"Kentucky politicians told the story for years," Klotter said. "Of course, it's not true. But it does show how important local politics was to people. It also says something about what politicians will say to win elections."

Fess was in the army during the Spanish-American War of 1898. Roosevelt, president from 1901 to 1909, was the conflict's great hero. The Battle of San Juan Hill, near Santiago, Cuba, grabbed headlines.

Whitaker was a cook who got no closer to combat than Florida, according to Klotter and William T. Cornett, the latter the author of a story about Fess that appeared in the *Kentucky Explorer* magazine in 1991. Fess did serve with the Rough Riders, but after the war, Klotter added.

Nonetheless, Fess swore that he took a Spanish slug at San Juan Hill. In *History of Corporal Fess Whitaker*, his 1918 autobiography, the jailer-judge explained:

> *Teddy, without a wound and I with a bullet wound in my left arm, took me by the hand and said: "Fess: we have gained a great battle for our country. You or I will be the next President of the United States, and if you get the nomination I am for you, and if I get the nomination I want you to be for me, for you have great influence in the United States."*

Cornett, whose article was reprinted from a 1988 issue of the *Whitesburg Mountain Eagle* newspaper, wrote that Fess understood that "a stirring service record could only help a candidate…He also knew that embellishing the record a little wouldn't hurt, either."

So Fess recounted the story over and over. Eventually, the myth became a staple in the story bag of Kentucky politicians, great and small.

After serving as county jailer from 1917 to 1921, Fess tossed his hat in the ring for county judge. When he was declared the winner, Fess was locked in his own jail, possibly for dumping a pitcher of buttermilk on the outgoing judge but "definitely for public drunkenness," Cornett wrote. "Jailed Jailer Elected Judge of Letcher County," *Louisville Courier-Journal* headlines trumpeted.

Fess's fable survived long after a car crash cut his life short in 1927. Whitaker was forty-seven, the first Letcher Countian to die in an auto accident, according to Cornett. Six years later, Whitaker's son became the first person from Letcher County to perish in an airplane crash, Cornett added.

In his article, he also quoted the whole story Fess told about his fateful meeting with Teddy Roosevelt after the Rough Riders charged up San Juan Hill:

> *Now that battle was a rough 'un. We had a hard time of it, but we won. My commander was none other than Teddy Roosevelt, and me and him got to be good friends. When the battle was over and the smoke was clearing, it just so happened that we reined our horses up together.*
>
> *Old Teddy looked out over the scene, and said, "Fess, my boy, we've won a great victory today." I said right back, "Lord, don't I know it." And Teddy went on: "This is going to make one of us President some day. Now, if you get the nomination, I'll vote for you, and if I get it I want you to promise me you'll do the same." I told him if he got it I would, but I also told him I didn't want to be no President all I want to be is jailer of Letcher County.*

"Honest Dick"

State Treasurer Dick Tate liked his nickname. "Honest Dick" seemed appropriate for a man who was guardian of the public purse for more than twenty years. But there's not a single monument to Tate anywhere in Frankfort, the Kentucky capital. That's because he allegedly embezzled more than $247,000 in state funds before disappearing in 1888.

"Nobody ever found out what became of him," Klotter said. "It's one of the greatest mysteries in Kentucky history."

The Tate affair was one of the greatest scandals, too. "Such a flash of lightning, and a peal of thunder, as was never before seen or heard came out of a clear sky, and rocked the state as nothing had done since the [Civil] war," a contemporary declared, according to *Kentucky: Decades of Discord, 1865–1900* by Klotter and historian Hambleton Tapp.

Klotter and Tapp added, "The episode had been like a nightmare… Almost overnight the people of the state seemed to suspect and distrust state officials and clamored for circumscription of their powers."

Kentuckians got their wish with the 1891 constitution. The new charter limited treasurers and other constitutional officers to just one term in office. "'Honest Dick' cast a pretty long shadow," commented Klotter.

Few figures in Kentucky history were more shadowy than James W. Tate, who was born near Frankfort in 1831. A Democrat, he was elected state treasurer in 1867. Almost routinely, voters returned Tate to office every two years through 1887. "Because he had apparently been such an outstanding treasurer, people started calling him 'Honest Dick,'" Klotter said.

Tate was last seen in Frankfort on March 14, 1888. He said he was going to Louisville on a short trip.

Klotter noted that "Honest Dick" allegedly spent two nights in Louisville, where he supposedly took in a stage show. Afterward, he reputedly left the state on a train bound for Cincinnati.

On March 20, an embarrassed Governor Simon Bolivar Buckner announced that "Honest Dick" had been suspended from office. Auditors had discovered that Tate's books didn't balance, not by a long shot.

Buckner said Tate pilfered $247,128.50, according to the *Kentucky Encyclopedia*. "But it is unknown how much he took with him when he fled the state," Klotter acknowledged.

Klotter and Tapp wrote that a clerk in Tate's office claimed that he spied the treasurer on March 14 with a large roll of bills, a coin purse, which he pocketed, and "two tobacco sacks filled with gold and silver coin."

Klotter guesses that Tate left with about $100,000. "But it was hard to tell because there had been no real auditing of his office for years. People simply trusted him."

Investigators found that Tate had mixed his and the state's money. According to Klotter and Tapp:

> *In the treasury vaults were found purses, beaded bags and other family effects. A little satchel purse, containing pieces of silver and gold, which had belonged to a deceased child, was discovered along with objects belonging to the state.*

Tate also loaned state money to important Kentucky officials. In 1872, Klotter and Tapp wrote, he advanced Governor Preston H. Leslie $5,000.

Ultimately, Tate was removed from office and indicted in absentia for embezzlement. "He evidently used state money to speculate in stocks and to buy land in other states and coal mines in Kentucky," Klotter said.

Where Tate went from Cincinnati—if he really got there—is unknown. But he did leave behind a wife and a daughter.

Supposedly, Tate was in Canada, then Japan and China. Allegedly, he returned from Asia to California and then showed up in South America. "He had written his family," Klotter said. "But the last letters came from Brazil."

The letters stopped in 1890. "Did he quit writing because he was afraid he could be traced through the letters?" Klotter wondered. "Or did he slip back into the United States under an assumed name? Nobody knows."

"DOUBLE-DISTILLED COWARDLY RUFFIANISM"

The Reverend Elisha Green was "the unknown Rosa Parks," according to a former Maysville Community College English professor. "Reverend Green refused to give up his seat long before Rosa Parks did," George Vaughn said. "She held fast to what she believed and he did, too."

An African American seamstress, Parks helped doom segregation when she refused to leave a white-only section of a Montgomery, Alabama bus. The 1955 incident helped spark the modern American civil rights movement.

A Bourbon County–born ex-slave and Baptist minister, Green didn't budge when three white men demanded his seat and beat him on a Maysville–Paris train in 1883. "He just decided he'd given up enough," said Vaughn, who played a seventy-year-old Green in the *Kentucky Chautauqua*, a series of dramatic performances about notable Kentuckians sponsored by the Lexington-based Kentucky Humanities Council.

"Green had to give up his son, who was sold as a slave down the river," Vaughn said.

> *He never saw his son again. Then Green saw the end of slavery but the beginning of segregation, which seemed like a return to slavery. He simply wasn't going to sit by and watch things go back the way they were.*

Green had the man who led the attack, the Reverend G.T. Gould, charged with assault and battery. He also sued him for $300. An all-white jury in Paris, the Bourbon County seat, found Gould guilty but awarded Green only $24. "It was a little victory, but a victory anyway," Vaughn said.

Green became an ordained minister before the Civil War when he also borrowed enough money to buy freedom for himself, his wife and two daughters. He was unable to prevent the sale of his son, Vaughn said.

After the war, Green organized Baptist churches in Bourbon, Mason and Fleming Counties. He lived in Maysville and regularly rode the train to Paris, where he preached. The pastor wasn't expecting trouble when he bought a ticket and boarded the train at Maysville on June 8, 1883.

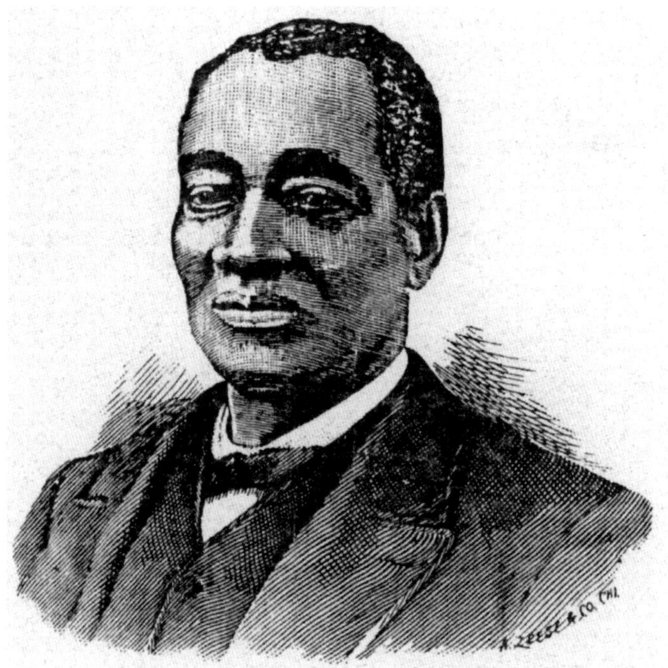

Reverend Elisha W. Green. *Courtesy of the Kentucky Gateway Museum.*

When the train made its regular stop at Millersburg, a group of whites got on, including Gould, who was president of Millersburg Female College, Professors Bristow and Carrington and some students. There were plenty of empty seats, Vaughn said.

But Gould and the two professors ordered Green to move, taunting him with racial epithets. In his autobiography, *Life of the Rev. Elisha W. Green*, Green said that he would have relinquished his seat "if I had been asked politely, and if there had been other seats in the car…"

Gould and Carrington pinned the sixty-five-year-old Green. Green said Bristow beat him over the head with "a brass bound valise." Green, who had been crippled in a railroad accident many years before, suffered cuts on his head and fingers. He might have been hurt worse had the conductor not stopped the attack, Vaughn said.

The *Maysville New Republican* rallied to Green, describing the attack as "double-distilled cowardly ruffianism that we would not have believed any Kentuckian had been guilty of….It is a shocking and disgusting outrage when we consider that the attack was made upon a colored man, and we are of the firm belief that it never would have been attempted if he (Green) had been white."

Gould denied that he and the two professors hurt Green. Green, who died at age seventy-eight in 1893, described Gould as "an educated dude of a white man that can lie faster than the Recording Angel in heaven would have patience to write." The pastor added, "There is an expression which says: 'A lie can go a mile while truth is putting his boots on.'"

"The Voice of Organized Labor"

If the Kentucky labor movement had a founding father, it probably was James McGill. The Louisville union official and labor newspaper publisher started the Kentucky State Federation of Labor and was the organization's first president. "McGill recognized that Kentucky workers needed a statewide organization to deal with their problems, especially in lobbying for labor legislation," explains *Labor History in Kentucky*, a book that the state Department of Education published for schoolteachers in 1986.

McGill, whose paper was called the *Journal of Labor*, traveled the state, meeting with local unions and urging them to band together. But Covington and Louisville labor groups emerged as rivals for a charter from the American Federation of Labor, whose president was the famous union leader Samuel Gompers.

In January 1900, the United Trades and Labor Assembly and its supporters founded a state body in Covington. Soon after, forty delegates "from various labor organizations throughout the State" joined the Louisville Central Labor Union in starting their own federation, the *Louisville Courier-Journal* reported.

"National President Gompers, according to McGill, has written a letter saying that the body formed at Louisville will be the one to receive his charter," the *Courier-Journal* said. "At any rate, a lively controversy between the rival bodies is very certain to ensue."

Besides electing McGill president, the new KSFL voted to hold its first state convention at Central City in October 1901.

Delegates also established the KSFL's headquarters in Louisville and approved a resolution "denouncing the labor men who recently formed a State Federation at Covington," the *Courier-Journal* said. In addition, KSFL leaders urged Gompers to acknowledge their assembly "as the legal body in Kentucky."

Though Gompers recognized the KSFL, internal strife continued to plague the organization. "At one point, the charter was revoked by the national AFL and then reissued in 1905, but by 1910, the disputes had been resolved and the organization was firmly established," according to *Labor History in Kentucky*. As a result, wrote Joseph Krislov in the *Kentucky Encyclopedia*, the KSFL "became the voice of organized labor" in Kentucky.

The basic principles upon which the KSFL was founded still guide its eventual successor, the Kentucky State AFL-CIO, according to President Bill Londrigan. "We strive for more than better pay, benefits and working conditions for union members," said Londrigan, who is based in Frankfort. "We in the union movement want to help make a better world for everybody who works for a living."

The "Lyin' Tree"

The old "Lyin' Tree" that shaded politicians from the hot Fancy Farm sun was either a victim of divine punishment or too much of a good thing.

"It depends on who's telling the tale," said Bob Spalding, who was chairman of the famous Fancy Farm political picnic. "Governor Louie Nunn said that too much fertilizer would kill anything. Other people said that the Lord killed the tree with a bolt of lightning because He was tired of hearing all the lying that went on under it."

For the record, the 133-year-old red oak succumbed to lightning, heaven-sent or otherwise, on April 15, 1974. So says a small gray granite memorial that marks where the tree grew in Fancy Farm, a historic old

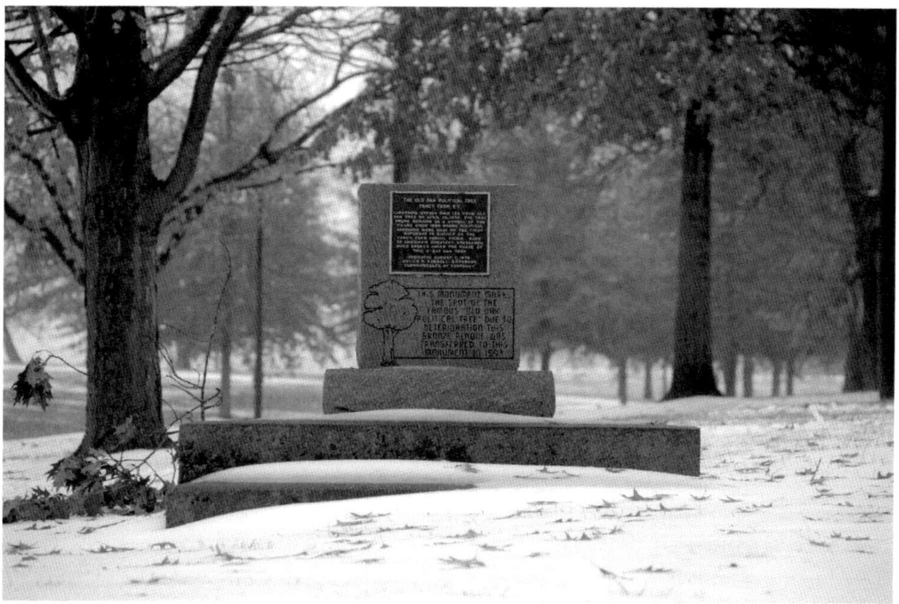

"The Lyin' Tree," Fancy Farm, Kentucky (Graves County).

western Kentucky Catholic community of about four hundred souls in Graves County.

"They used to say that nobody who didn't speak at Fancy Farm picnic ever got elected governor," Spalding said. "For almost one hundred years, they all spoke under that old tree that was nicknamed 'The Lyin' Tree.'"

Fancy Farm hosts the state's best-known political picnic. The all-day affair features barbecue and bombast, usually as warm as the weather.

After it was gone, the Lyin' Tree wasn't forgotten. Politicians and pundits praised it; a ten-foot section of the tree's storm-shattered trunk was preserved. "They covered what was left of the tree with concrete, added white paint and put a bronze tablet on it telling about the tree," Spalding said.

But the trunk gradually rotted from within. "In 1993, they took it down because they were afraid it would fall and hurt somebody," Spalding explained. "That's when they put up the stone marker."

The plaque was preserved as part of the marker. "Some of America's greatest orators have spoken under the shade of this great oak tree," it reads.

Spalding ranks Vice President Alben Barkley as the greatest. "He was born and raised in Wheel, seven or eight miles from here," Spalding said.

Eventually, Barkley settled in Paducah, became a lawyer and got into Democratic politics. He climbed the ladder from U.S. representative to Senate majority leader and vice president. He was reelected to the Senate after he was vice president.

Another Paducah Democrat, Governor Julian M. Carroll, dedicated the plaque and the Lyin' Tree's concrete carcass at the 1976 Fancy Farm picnic. *Louisville Courier-Journal* columnist Ed Ryan reported that the oak was "critically wounded…by a nonpartisan bolt of lightning and never recovered.

At the 1979 picnic, Nunn, who was from Glasgow, told a different version of the tree's demise. He suggested that the tree had been poisoned by an excess of political oratory, claiming "too much fertilizer will kill anything."

Shaded by two strapping young maples, the Lyin' Tree memorial is on the grassy front lawn of the old red brick St. Jerome's school. "The crowds got so big that we had to move the political speaking around back by the picnic ground," Spalding said. "But under this stone lies the grave of old-time Kentucky political rhetoric."